Praise for *Employee Engangement*

"Macc   a pr   analy   engagement   y it wo   impo   , how to
create and   engaged worforce."

  Fritz Drasgow, *University of Illinois at Urbana-Champaign*

"*Employee Engagement* walks us through the complexity of this deceptively simple concept and makes concrete the process of translating engagement into hard f   ults."

  Peter Cappelli, *The Wharton School, University of Pennsylvania*

"A hugely important topic, handled with just the right mix of scholarly insight and practical experience. This book is a valuable addition to the literature."

  Jeffery S. Schippmann, *Balfour Beatty Construction*

"If you want to increase employee engagement to achieve your organization's strategic objectives this is the book for you. It deconstructs what engagement really means, explains what factors shape it, shows how to diagnose your organization current state and tell you what managerial levers you can use to increase it and consequently raise organizational performance. This book is at once scientifically sound and highly readable."

  Michael Beer, *Harvard Business School*

"No one knows more about employee engagement, in all its forms, than do these authors. They give careful, useful and practical advice on using employee opinion surveys to measure and increase employee engagement!"

  Allen I. Kraut, *Baruch College, C.U.N.Y.*

Talent Management Essentials

Series Editor: Steven G. Rogelberg, PhD
Professor and Director Organizational Science, University of North Carolina – Charlotte

Senior Advisory Board:
- Eric Elder, PhD, Director, Talent Management, Corning Incorporated
- William H. Macey, PhD, Chief Executive Officer, Valtera Corporation
- Cindy McCauley, PhD, Senior Fellow, Center for Creative Leadership
- Elaine Pulakos, PhD, Chief Operating Officer, PDRI, a PreVisor Company
- Douglas H. Reynolds, PhD, Vice President, Assessment Technology, Development Dimensions International
- Ann Marie Ryan, PhD, Professor, Michigan State University
- Lise Saari, PhD, Director, Global Workforce Research, IBM
- John Scott, PhD, Vice President, Applied Psychological Techniques, Inc.
- Dean Stamoulis, PhD, Managing Director, Executive Assessment Practice Leader for the Americas, Russell Reynolds Associates

Special Features

Each volume contains a host of actual case studies, sample materials, tips, and cautionary notes. Issues pertaining to globalization, technology, and key executive points are highlighted throughout.

Titles in the Talent Management Essentials series:

Employee Engagement:

Tools for Analysis, Practice, and Competitive Advantage

William H. Macey,
Benjamin Schneider,
Karen M. Barbera, and
Scott A. Young

WILEY-BLACKWELL

A John Wiley & Sons, Ltd., Publication

This edition first published 2009
© Valtera Corporation

Blackwell Publishing was acquired by John Wiley & Sons in February 2007. Blackwell's publishing program has been merged with Wiley's global Scientific, Technical, and Medical business to form Wiley-Blackwell.

Registered Office
John Wiley & Sons Ltd, The Atrium, Southern Gate, Chichester, West Sussex, PO19 8SQ, United Kingdom

Editorial Offices
350 Main Street, Malden, MA 02148–5020, USA
9600 Garsington Road, Oxford, OX4 2DQ, UK
The Atrium, Southern Gate, Chichester, West Sussex, PO19 8SQ, UK

For details of our global editorial offices, for customer services, and for information about how to apply for permission to reuse the copyright material in this book please see our website at www.wiley.com/wiley-blackwell.

The right of William H. Macey, Benjamin Schneider, Karen M. Barbera, and Scott A. Young to be identified as the authors of this work has been asserted in accordance with the Copyright, Designs and Patents Act 1988.

Wiley also publishes its books in a variety of electronic formats. Some content that appears in print may not be available in electronic books.

Designations used by companies to distinguish their products are often claimed as trademarks. All brand names and product names used in this book are trade names, service marks, trademarks or registered trademarks of their respective owners. The publisher is not associated with any product or vendor mentioned in this book. This publication is designed to provide accurate and authoritative information in regard to the subject matter covered. It is sold on the understanding that the publisher is not engaged in rendering professional services. If professional advice or other expert assistance is required, the services of a competent professional should be sought.

Library of Congress Cataloging-in-Publication Data

Employee engagement : tools for analysis, practice, and competitive advantage /
William H. Macey ... [et al.].
    p. cm. – (Talent management essentials)
    Includes bibliographical references and index.
    ISBN 978-1-4051-7903-4 (hardcover : alk. paper) – ISBN 978-1-4051-7902-7 (pbk. : alk. paper)   1. Employee motivation.   2. Employees–Attitudes.   I. Macey, William H.
    HF5549.5.M63E47   2009
    658.3′14–dc22

2008054917

A catalogue record for this book is available from the British Library.

Icon in Case Scenario boxes © Kathy Konkle / istockphoto.com

Set in 10.5 on 12.5 pt Minion by SNP Best-set Typesetter Ltd., Hong Kong
Printed and bound in Singapore by Ho Printing Singapore Pte Ltd

2   2010

For George and our family – Bill, Todd, Lauren, Katherine, Amanda, and Billy (WHM)

For Jack Bartlett, mentor, friend and The Great Engager (BS)

For Michael and Carter, who give meaning to all I do (KB)

For my wife Jennifer and our three amazing girls, Hannah, Carly, and Kayla (SY)

Contents

Series Editor's Preface

The *Talent Management Essentials* series presents state-of-the-art thinking on critical talent management topics ranging from global staffing, to career pathing, to engagement, to executive staffing, to performance management, to mentoring, to real-time leadership development. Authored by leading authorities and scholars on their respective topics, each volume offers state-of-the-art thinking and the epitome of evidence-based practice. These authors bring to their books an incredible wealth of experience working with small, large, public, and private organizations, as well as keen insights into the science and best practices associated with talent management.

Written succinctly and without superfluous "fluff," this series provides powerful and practical treatments of essential talent topics critical to maximizing individual and organizational health, well-being, and effectiveness. The books, taken together, provide a comprehensive and contemporary treatment of approaches, tools, and techniques associated with Talent Management. The goal of the series is to produce focused, prescriptive volumes that translate the data- and practice-based knowledge of organizational psychology, human resources management, and organizational behavior into practical, "how to" advice for dealing with cutting-edge organizational issues and problems.

Talent Management Essentials is a comprehensive, practitioner-oriented series of "best practices" for the busy solution-oriented manager, executive, HR leader, and consultant. And, in its application of evidence-based practice, this series will also appeal to professors, executive MBA students, and graduate students in Organizational Behavior, Human Resources Management, and I/O Psychology.

Steven Rogelberg

Preface

Rarely has a term that represents a "soft" topic resonated as strongly with business executives as employee engagement has in recent years. Part of the reason is likely an increased focus on human capital as a source of competitive advantage. As technology has quickly reduced or eliminated many operational sources of competitive advantage, the focus has shifted to human capital as an avenue to competitive advantage that is difficult to imitate.

In addition, the early part of this decade saw enormous increases in layoffs; "do more with less" was the mantra heard by employees in countless corporations. Executives in many organizations were not only looking for ways to increase the productivity of their workforces, but were also attempting to accomplish this with a leaner staff. Thus, much of the interest in employee engagement stems from a general concern for productivity. Further contributing to the interest are general concerns about the viability of today's workforce, particularly given the seeming lack of a long-term commitment by companies to their employees and the simultaneous control employees have taken for their work lives.[1]

This interest has led to a flood of ideas about what can be done to harness the "discretionary" effort of employees. The essential notion underlying these ideas is that employees will be more likely to direct their efforts toward things that matter for company success if they receive more of what management thinks will satisfy employees. Consistent with this line of thought, it has become common to regard concepts such as employee satisfaction and employee engagement as equivalent. We take issue with that view and make it clear why such an approach leads organizations to misdirect both their time and resources.

Thus, this book takes a dramatically different approach and shows how satisfaction differs from engagement. Whereas satisfaction represents contentment or satiation, we define engagement in terms that connote energy and provide a simple and compelling set of principles on which any organization can create and sustain a more engaged workforce. Going further, we give practical guidance on how to establish the kind of culture that both drives and sustains engagement.

It is important to recognize that engagement is not about a zero-sum game of getting more from employees at less cost. Rather, focusing on employee engagement means facing the challenge of how both organizations and employees can simultaneously benefit – a "win-win" scenario of enhanced organizational effectiveness coupled with heightened employee well-being. It is our conviction that both are not only achievable but likely when a well-designed engagement campaign is defined and executed. In the chapters that follow we provide the essential background in concept and practice for HR professionals, management consultants, and others who advise organizations on how to achieve the full benefits of competitive advantage through employee engagement.

Acknowledgments

Our thoughts on engagement reflect an exciting journey that has been shared with our colleagues, whose insights, contributions, and research partnership have been instrumental in shaping our views. First, we wish to acknowledge our colleagues at Valtera who have helped us to frame our views on engagement, create diagnostic measures to assess it, and conduct the research to show how an engaged workforce does in fact lead to competitive advantage. In particular, we would like to thank Holly Lam and Wayne Lee in this regard. We would also like to thank our colleagues at Valtera for their support while writing this book, as well for the dedication and professionalism they bring to every client interaction. The relationships that they forge allow us the opportunity to continue to consult with and learn from so many excellent organizations. Our journey also has been shared with our colleagues in the client organizations with whom we are so proud to partner, and in particular Karen Paul of 3M, and Alan Colquitt and David Futrell of Eli Lilly and Company. Our clients have challenged our thoughts, given us new insights, and provided us with practical and compelling examples of how engagement matters. Special thanks must go as well to the following individuals for so willingly sharing with us their experiences in implementing employee engagement initiatives in their companies as we prepared this book: Nigel Martin, VP of HR, Harrah's Entertainment, Inc.; Terry Seamons, Senior VP of HR, Entergy; Angela Lalor, Sr. VP of HR, 3M; Anthony Murphy, Sr. VP of HR, Eli Lilly and Company; and Carl Walker, Sr. VP of HR, North America, Huhtamaki.

We need to express particular thanks to Jennifer Stoll, Laura O'Shea, Laura Schiff, and Saifee Doriwala who helped with creating the manuscript including editing and graphics. Without their energy we wouldn't have been able to finish the project. Special thanks are also due to Steven Rogelberg for his help and patience throughout the process and to an anonymous reviewer whose suggestions greatly helped to improve the book. We were fortunate to have such excellent help and advice as this project unfolded but need to state with certainty that we are completely responsible for any errors that remain.

Certainly most important is for us to acknowledge the support and encouragement of our families, who we know got much less attention than they deserved during this period. Bill is particularly grateful to George for her patience and support during a time when she faced a most daunting challenge of her own with remarkable courage.

About the Authors

William H. Macey is CEO of Valtera and has 30 years of experience consulting with organizations to design and implement survey research programs. He has served as an advisor to the Mayflower Group since 1992 and is the co-author of several recent publications on employee engagement. He is a Fellow of SIOP, APA, and APS and is a SIOP past president. He received his PhD from Loyola University Chicago in 1975.

Benjamin Schneider is Senior Research Fellow at Valtera and Professor Emeritus of the University of Maryland. He has won Distinguished Scientific Contributions Awards both in Psychology and Marketing, he has published nine books and more than 140 journal articles and book chapters. He has also consulted widely with many Fortune 100 companies especially on issues concerning organizational service climate and employee engagement, and the way these link to customer satisfaction and financial success.

Karen M. Barbera is a Managing Principal at Valtera Corporation, responsible for overseeing the practice group focused on employee engagement surveys and organizational diagnostics. She consults with numerous Fortune 100 level companies on the design, execution, and use of employee surveys to drive organizational improvement efforts, including the delivery of C-suite presentations of results. She is also the principal author of Valtera's feedback and action planning programs. She received her PhD in industrial and organizational psychology from Bowling Green State University.

Scott A. Young is a Managing Consultant at Valtera Corporation. He consults with the firm's organizational survey clients on content development and measurement, reporting and interpretation of results, research, and action planning. In addition, he has consulted with clients on multirater feedback and employee selection, and oversees the development of Valtera's proprietary employee survey normative data and research. He received his PhD in industrial and organizational psychology from Northern Illinois University.

Chapter 1

Engaging Engagement

Employee engagement is an engaging notion – we get excited by it, we get involved in it, we're willing to invest time and effort in it, and we get proactive about pursuing it – that's why you are reading this book. Engagement implies something special – something at least a bit out of the ordinary and maybe even exceptional. Moreover, it sounds like something maybe too good to be true, both for employee and employer. Many would envy those who are so absorbed in their work that time flies, who seem passionate about their work, who find meaning and challenge in their jobs, and frankly, who simply look forward to coming to work every day. It just seems like the kind of job that we all deserve – indeed, it's what people expect when they start a new job. At the same time, we envy the organization where employees are focused, passionate, and want to be there and who are innovative, proactive, and do the right things the right ways. It's no wonder then that some of the most admired business leaders speak wistfully about engagement, and see it as essential to organizational success. As Jack and Suzy Welch suggest: "Employee engagement first. It goes without saying that no company, small or large, can win over the long run without energized employees who believe in the mission and understand how to achieve it."[1]

How Engagement Makes a Difference and What Engagement Is

The general thinking on the notion is that engaged employees give more of what they have to offer, and that as a result, an engaged workforce is simply a more productive one. In her testimony before the US Congress, workforce pundit Tamara Erickson said: "Improving engagement – finding ways to encourage individuals to invest more psychic energy in work – is the single most powerful lever that corporations have to improve productivity."[2]

That's a powerful statement and it raises difficult questions: Does a more highly engaged workforce truly produce superior performance in organizations? Just what is psychic energy? And just as importantly, how does the corporation create or release that energy?

The Business Case for Employee Engagement

The claims being made for engagement are substantial. If employees are more engaged their organizations should demonstrate superior financial performance, the ultimate metric against which success and failure is judged. We have good evidence from some of our research of that potential and it is shown in Figure 1.1. There, we show how employee engagement across companies is reflected in three different indices of financial performance.

We had employees in 65 firms in different industries complete our engagement index and then for each company we averaged the data from their employees. Then we asked the following question: If you take the top and bottom 25 percent of the companies on the engagement index and look at the financial consequences what are the results?

You can see in Figure 1.1 that for Return on Assets (ROA), Profitability (actually profits divided by revenues), and Shareholder Value the differences are quite dramatic with shareholder value being more than doubled. Shareholder value was calculated using an approach commonly used in financial research.[3]

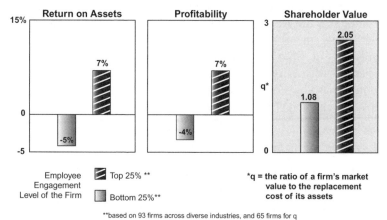

Figure 1.1 Engagement and financial performance

Good to Know:

Shareholder Value as a Measure of Engagement Impact

One challenge in evaluating the impact of an HR initiative is the choice of the outcome measure. All measures are not equal; their interpretation is often clouded by differences within and between organizations. For example, accounting measures (like ROA) are generally not comparable across firms or at least industries. This makes it difficult to evaluate the impact of a program on the competitive advantages that accrue, for example, to an engaged workforce since such evaluation by definition requires a comparison between companies.

In contrast with accounting-based measures, measures of shareholder value are forward-looking and cumulative. An appropriate measure of shareholder value allows for comparability across firms and industries. Most important, the cumulative and forward-looking nature of share-holder value means that it reflects anticipated and *sustainable* impact. It is sustainability that reflects the essential nature of competitive advantage.

Capital market measures of shareholder value, such as Tobin's q, reflect the value of the firm that has been created beyond the replacement costs of the firm's assets (that is, the ratio of the market value of the firm to the replacement cost of its assets). Thus, firms which have higher such ratios have greater anticipated market returns relative to the investments that have been made.

Figure 1.1 clearly shows that firms that achieve higher levels of employee engagement also create higher levels of shareholder value ... certainly good news for their investors and the executive teams who design and implement their strategies.

If an engaged workforce produces such dramatic financial outcomes how can we understand what this energy is that is associated with engagement? It turns out there are two kinds of energy: psychic energy – or what people personally experience – and behavioral energy – what is visible to others. At least as important is the question: What kinds of conditions can we create in the work place to foster such energy? We briefly describe each of these.

Engagement as Psychic Energy: On the Inside

Psychic energy brings to mind powerful images. Simply put, those who apply more psychic energy to a given task focus intensely on it and spend less energy focusing elsewhere. Common sense tells us that an organization that can capture more of that energy on the tasks that need doing in turn has a greater opportunity to create value.

Most of us have had the experience of being totally absorbed, totally focused on the task at hand. We use various expressions to refer to these moments, such as being "in the zone" or in "flow."[4] We think of these moments as peak experiences, and in that sense they are memorable and positive. The question of whether we are satisfied at the time simply doesn't arise because our attention isn't on being satisfied, it's focused on the task at hand. Most people can identify when they have such experiences and the common ingredient of those experiences: It happens when we have a clear objective or goal we are trying to attain, when we have a sense of urgency about completion, and when we put intense effort into attaining it.

It may have already struck you that if events like being "in the zone" are relatively uncommon, then the goal of creating an engaged workforce might be elusive. So, engagement is probably best thought of as something that comes in degrees, perhaps at the extreme levels representing being "in the zone," but without necessarily implying that engagement can only refer to such extreme moments.

We make this important point because engagement can be an important concept only to the extent that it is realistically sustainable. Being "in the zone" isn't ordinary. Nonetheless, the allure of the extreme is one that captures our imagination, and serves in the extreme as the defining nature of what engagement feels like.

It's the emphasis on energy that sets engagement apart from other popularized HR concepts, especially employee satisfaction. Employee satisfaction implies satiation and contentment with what has been obtained whereas engagement implies going after, seeking, and striving. We'll see later that it's a little bit trickier than this – primarily because of the way these different ideas about employees have been understood and measured. Nevertheless the notion of energy is key to engagement whereas satiation is the key to understanding satisfaction. With energy in mind, let's sketch out what it means to be psychologically engaged from an employee's view by imagining we are interviewing employees about it. For example:

- *Describe the feelings of enthusiasm, focus, and being energized.* "Work doesn't feel tiring, but exhilarating. I feel a sense of enthusiasm for what I do. I feel a sense of self-efficacy, not self-satisfaction, but of vitality and competence that comes from doing something that I personally value. I see myself as part of the vitality of the organization, as a significant contributor to accomplishing organizational goals."
- *Tell me how absorbed you feel in your work.* "I frequently have the sense of being lost in time, as 'suspended' in the present. I find that I am fully involved in my work. I am very attentive to what I am doing and do not suffer from distractions."
- *So, are you saying you are more focused?* "Good question. I feel fully absorbed and aware of my place in relationship to my co-workers and what they and the organization are trying to do."

Engagement is the psychic kick of immersion, striving, absorption, focus, and involvement. In its fullest form it is not a usual sensation for if it were we would not obsess about how to achieve it. But engagement is not only psychic energy felt and sensed by employees; it is observable in behavior.

Engagement as Behavioral Energy: How Engagement Looks to Others

Engagement is visible to others in the form of behavior and we want to focus in on that behavior because, ultimately, this is what produces results. Importantly, we know that employees can serve as effective and valid reporters of what is going on in the organization. So, it's helpful to think of what an engaged workforce looks like to those who actually do the work inside the organization. We're going to go into some detail about what behavioral engagement looks like. We do this because it is sometimes like other notions of behavior we have but it is more than those. For example, some speak about commitment to the organization and involvement in one's work but if that's all it is, then it seems we could stop right here, because much has been written about those topics. It's precisely because engagement captures something different – something more – that we need to find a level of precision in our thinking and expression that distinguishes engagement from those concepts. As we'll see later, thinking about engagement in the ways it is different can lead us to a path less traveled, one with very different consequences for the organization.

Here is what an engaged workforce looks like:

- Employees will think and work proactively: Engaged employees anticipate opportunities to take action – and actually do take action – in ways that are aligned with organizational goals.
- They will expand their own thinking about what is necessary as job demands shift and expand their roles to match these new demands: Engaged employees aren't tied to a job description. Rather, they are focused on the goals they are trying to achieve and that are consistent with the success of the organization. Doing something more or different isn't the question; it's a matter of doing what's necessary without thinking of whether what's necessary is part of the job.
- Employees actively find ways to expand their own skills in a way that is consistent with what's important to their roles and organizational mission: Engaged employees take ownership for their personal development not just for their own sake but so that they can contribute more effectively. Employees see their own self-interest in skill development as consistent with what is good for the organization but they do more than think about this, they do it. So, this self-development behavior isn't seen as a matter of ultimate self-sacrifice, but what makes sense in a relationship between employee and employer; engagement is not just about what I can get but what I can give.
- Employees persist – even when confronted with obstacles: Engagement matters most when things aren't easy to do, aren't going according to plan, and/or when situations are ambiguous and call

for a matter of trust on both sides. The reason why executives are so attracted to the notion of discretionary effort is that they recognize that all activity is not subject to management design or control, and that questions of motivation are quite difficult to address. What executives want are employees who don't need reminding or prodding, and who not only sense the need to get things done but do it, whether or not now is the convenient time or it is perfectly clear who should be doing it.

- They will adapt to change: A key characteristic of an engaged workforce is employees who adapt when circumstances require. This can take shape in different forms, but the key is that they respond to the uncertainty that is inherent in a changing business environment and they actively embrace change – indeed sometimes proactively suggest change.

We will expand on these component notions – both of what engagement looks like and what it feels like – in Chapter 2. For now, though, we offer the following working definition:

> Engagement is an individual's sense of purpose and focused energy, evident to others in the display of personal initiative, adaptability, effort, and persistence directed toward organizational goals.

Good to Know:
Engagement in a Talent Management Framework

Talent Management refers to those human capital systems that attract the right talent and leverage that talent in a way that achieves the greatest return from individual and collective employee capabilities. In addition to sourcing, recruitment, on-boarding, and selection, this embraces managing the employee–employer relationship including performance management and issues related to sustaining employee motivation. It is particularly out of concern for the latter and the desire to capture unrealized employee potential that engagement falls under the talent management umbrella. Perhaps less obvious, employee engagement addresses another focus of talent management, namely, the need for organizations to adapt quickly to changing conditions. A more engaged workforce is more adaptable and therefore can be deployed more readily and likely at lower overall costs.

How an Engaged Workforce Creates Positive Financial Consequences for Organizations

Earlier we made the business case for an engaged workforce. We showed (see Figure 1.1) how companies with an engaged workforce had superior ROA, profitability, and more than double the shareholder value if they were in the top 25 percent compared to the bottom 25 percent on engagement of the companies we studied. Since then we have been outlining the attributes of an engaged workforce in terms of the psychic and behavioral energy we can expect from engaged employees. But that energy itself of course does not translate directly into the financial outcomes we showed are *related* to that energy. Obviously there is a process whereby the translation into financial outcomes occurs. This process is our focus here because it has direct consequences for the kinds of conditions that must exist for: (a) employees to feel and be engaged; and (b) produce the financial consequences hoped for. Look at Figure 1.2 as we describe this process and focus in for now on the second and third boxes, the ones labeled "Employee engagement feelings" and "Employee engagement behaviors." We'll deal with the "High performance work environment" in the far left of the figure later.

Figure 1.2 presents a schematic overview of how we conceptualize engagement with both its antecedents and its consequences. The

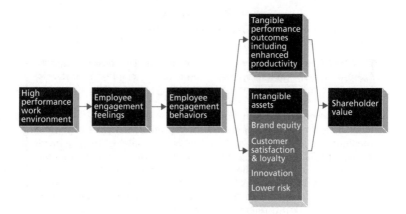

Figure 1.2 Employee engagement value chain

antecedents are in the work environment and we refer to and think of such a work environment as one that facilitates, permits, and allows employees to be engaged. Engagement has two important facets, one psychological and the other behavioral. The psychological has all to do with the way people feel – focused, intense, enthusiastic – and the behavioral has all to do with what they do – they are persistent, adaptable, and proactive. As shown in Figure 1.2, engagement provides the bases for creating tangible outcomes such as enhanced performance, and a set of intangible assets including customer loyalty, intellectual capital, and brand image rarely addressed in human resources and human capital writings. Also, engagement serves to lower the risk profile of the organization. This happens because employees are more dedicated to creating value for the company, more consistent in their interactions with customers and other stakeholders, and less likely to leave the organization. All these in turn impact cash flow and ultimately shareholder value.[5] What we want to emphasize in particular is the role of employee engagement in creating the *intangible* assets shown in Figure 1.2 and thereby lowering risk, both of which extend far beyond the implications of greater productivity generically defined to create shareholder value.

We want readers to think strategically about these engagement components and to see that the engagement components and their relationships to productivity, intangible assets, and risk reduction constitute a strategic mapping process not unlike those advocated by Kaplan and Norton in their important book *Strategy Maps*.[6] These models essentially provide an action plan for converting intangible assets into shareholder value.

Executives are more adept and comfortable in mapping the marketing and operational elements of their business strategies. They struggle with the human capital components of their strategies because they do not grasp how human issues map to the intangible assets they do understand – brand, customer loyalty, and innovation. There is a very large gap in thinking about how to move from the high performance work environment practices we will talk about next and these outcomes. As a result, the logic of cause and effect relationships – if I do X then Y is likely to follow – breaks down for a lack of rigor in thinking about the steps between engagement and ultimate outcomes like shareholder value.

As we shall see later in greater detail, the linkages shown in Figure 1.2 are supported by a significant body of research originating in multiple disciplines, including psychology, economics, and marketing. What is critical here is recognizing how engagement serves as the missing link between a high performance work environment and both the tangible outcomes and intangible assets that in turn create shareholder value. The concept of engagement offers us an opportunity to look inside the "black box" to see what the human assets that work for us feel and do and how that creates the ultimate competitive advantage for firms.

On High Performance Work Environments: Four Principles for Creating an Engaged Workforce

Now we can focus on the far left column in Figure 1.2 because something needs to get this process to unfold in the right ways. These high performance work practices address four key factors, each of which relates to what we consider a fundamental principle of engagement. Specifically, engagement follows when:

- employees have the capacity to engage;
- employees have a reason or the motivation to engage;
- employees have the freedom to engage; and
- employees know how to engage.

We now consider each in turn.

The Capacity to Engage

Do employees possess the goal-directed energy and the resilience to maintain that energy when faced with the usual obstacles to goal attainment? This energy flows from the sense of competence and self-sufficiency that all people desire, though certainly some are more self-directed than others. Engagement follows naturally out of the motivation people have for autonomy and competence.[7] Organizations *contribute to* and *facilitate* this energy by giving employees the information they need to do their jobs well, by giving learning opportunities and feedback so they can develop self-confidence, and by supporting employees in their efforts to renew their personal energy levels through a balance between work and their personal lives. Thus, our first principle of engagement is:

> Engagement requires a work environment that does not just demand "more" but promotes information sharing, provides learning opportunities, and fosters a balance in people's lives, thereby creating the bases for sustained energy and personal initiative.

Good to Know:
Is Engagement a Bottomless Reservoir to be Tapped?

Engagement is a powerful concept because it captures the notion of employees who give it their all, work with passion, or who go the extra mile. In this view, competitive advantage results from getting more from the available (human) resources.

This characterization of engagement is decidedly unbalanced – and therefore unsustainable. It implies that engagement is about one side getting more out of the other – which is unjust and therefore runs counter to a foundation of engagement: just and fair treatment. The kind of environment that works well for engagement is one in which both employees' and the organization's interests are served in the long run.

The Motivation to Engage

People come to work to work at jobs. Most of people's time at work is spent working at their jobs. There must be a reason for employees to *fully* invest their energy during work time. To the degree that jobs are high on intrinsic interest they stimulate engagement. Jobs are intrinsically interesting when they are challenging, meaningful, and offer opportunities for decision-making and autonomy in designing not only what will be done but how it will be done.[8] Specific and difficult goals also create energy in people and the research is clear that these kinds of goals yield increased accomplishment at work.[9] The motivation to engage also follows from treating people with respect, and in so doing, showing they are valued and thereby establishing a basis for them to reciprocate through their voluntary engagement. This also follows when organization and employee values are aligned. Our second principle of engagement is:

Engagement happens when (a) employees have work that interests them and aligns with their values; and (b) employees are treated in a way that reinforces the natural tendency to reciprocate in kind.

Good to Know:
Engagement and the Employee Value Proposition

As management consultants, we're often asked about the relationship between Engagement and Talent Management. Because of the shifting demographics, there is an increased emphasis on talent acquisition and retention in most organizations. Retention, turnover and engagement topics are often mentioned in the same breath, and engagement often has been discussed as if the opposite – disengagement – implies turnover in the most extreme form. Indeed, some authors have directly positioned the engagement discussion in terms of the disengagement end of the continuum, and argue that by focusing on those factors that influence turnover one is simultaneously focusing on engagement.

In our opinion, this casual blending of questions regarding engagement and the employee value proposition (EVP) has had unfortunate consequences. The discussion of EVP is certainly an important one, and organizations will benefit greatly from building a superior employment brand (to drive attraction) and creating a work environment that minimizes unwanted turnover. However, the focus on what the employee *gets* from the "deal" misses the centrality of creating conditions for what the employee *gives back* – and that requires discussion of values alignment, jobs, and fair and just treatment as the bases of engagement and the creation of a high-engagement workforce.

The Freedom to Engage

It is when employees feel they have the freedom to take action – and that they will not be punished for doing so – that their initiative and being proactive becomes possible. Conversely, without that freedom to engage, there cannot be a link between the strategy of the firm and individual action, because feeling safe enough to take action doesn't psychologically exist.

Importantly, it is the times when it is most critical to the organization that people step up and make a difference that both organization and people are at risk. Hoping that individuals will sense the time and importance of taking action won't work if the risks of doing so require people to assume "hero" personas. It's unreasonable to expect adaptive and proactive behavior when they feel they are vulnerable – meaning they are without the support and safety of their manager and the organization. And how do they know this? They know this when they feel they have been treated fairly and that, in turn, leads them to trust. As we will see fairness is not a simple idea, nor is trust, but for now it is clear that fairness leads to trust and trust leads to feeling safe. Our third principle is:

> Engagement happens when people feel safe to take action on their own initiative. Consequently, trust matters most under conditions of adversity, ambiguity, and the need for change – *precisely when employee engagement is most important.*

The Focus of Strategic Engagement

Is energy channeled in a way that makes a difference? The foundation on which this understanding builds is the following idea: the *form* of engagement you want to drive is specific to the strategy and source of competitive advantage your company chooses. Just as there is a difference between a generic strategy and a strategic position,[10] there is a difference between a general level of engagement and the specific engagement behaviors that are essential to sustained competitive advantage *for you*. So, for example, have you chosen to be first in the marketplace with innovative products? You need your people to be engaged in innovation. Are you the service quality leader? You need your people to be engaged in service delivery excellence. We will address the strategic focus of engagement more completely in the next chapter but for now simply understand that strategy drives the specific kind of engagement you need and the way this is driven on a daily basis is by the kind of strategically focused work environment you create for your people.

Engagement "works" because employees see the direct connection between what they (should) do and organizationally beneficial outcomes. In the extreme form, engagement occurs when there is an alignment between the individual's goals and those of the organization. In situations where such is not the case, alignment processes are critical because they ensure that whatever motivational mechanism is in place (whether intrinsic or based on the principle of reciprocation), employee behaviors are those which are consistent with the

---

Best Practices and Realities:
Who Has Responsibility to Align Engagement with Strategy?

You might think that the answer to our question is obvious. The strategic implication of engagement suggests that it is the responsibility of senior leadership. The problem is that the environment can change so quickly that people need to adapt quickly and not always look immediately to leadership for the solution. As Angela Lalor, Senior Vice President of Human Resources at 3M told us, "it's not enough for people just to show up to work every day."[12] As she further noted, the problem is compounded by the size of the multinational organization so you can't rely on the expertise of individual leaders. People need to be comfortable with the rate of change and do their own adapting and aligning.

Ms. Lalor went on to explain that the only way to achieve this is by candidly sharing priorities and exposing as many people as possible to the planning process. Leaders at 3M do this by holding frequent employee meetings and through both systematic written communications, including personal emails from the CEO to the entire employee population, their internal website, leadership classes, and in employee orientation. These communication efforts are, as she puts it, "adult conversations" and fully intended to confront the reality of change. The communications emphasize what is happening in the marketplace and stress factors important to both customers and investors. The thrust of the 3M approach is that through engagement employees share in creating their own future rather than becoming victims of change. Importantly, the candor of these conversations is a model for creating the valid perception of trust and credibility that is a foundational element for building a culture of engagement.

So, the clear emphasis in 3M's approach is on holding leaders accountable for employee engagement. The HR team provides the tools, processes, and common language building the culture of engagement, but the individual supervisors and managers are the key to create engagement at the employee level. 3M establishes accountability by embedding engagement directly within their leadership competencies. They call it "Develops, Teaches, and Engages Others" and use it as a basis for yearly management assessments. 3M also provides managers with engagement scores from their company-wide opinion survey. So, feedback on employee engagement is an integral part of how they create competitive advantage.

organization's strategy.[11] As we progress, we'll see that alignment follows directly from creating the right kind of culture and continually monitoring and reinforcing it in all the nooks and crannies and at all levels within the organization. And creating that culture is not easy since it requires attention to a wide range of human capital issues ranging from who gets hired and how, to how they are brought on board and trained, and to what others around them make clear is the focus. It is because all of this is difficult to do that competitive advantage becomes possible for those who actually make it happen. This leads to our fourth principle:

> Strategic engagement happens when people know what the organization's strategic priorities are and why, and when the organization aligns its processes and practices – its culture – with attainment of those goals.

Engagement and Discretionary Effort

These four principles of engagement address the "discretionary" question – "why give that extra time and effort?" One answer is because "that's the deal," or the psychological contract between the individual and the organization. To the extent that the value proposition meets the needs of the employee, there is a reasonable basis for assuming that employees will perform at high levels consistent with their interpretation of the implicit contract. Engagement, in this view, is payback or reciprocation for what the company has provided. So, when the company provides opportunities for development, the right kinds of jobs, fair and just supervision, the right levels of pay and security, and so forth, engagement will follow because people fundamentally believe in reciprocation.

This perspective lends itself to significant distortion, as the discussion of engagement blends too easily into a discussion of satisfaction with the company overall, leadership, and specific elements of the deal. Nonetheless, the work environment plays a critical role in determining engagement, although perhaps less focused on individual satisfaction than the enabling and supportive elements of the work environment that allow the feelings of engagement and engagement behaviors to emerge.

Interaction of Cause and Effect

The four principles interact in complex ways to produce the fabric of engagement. So, some issues and tactics focus on the nature of work whereas other focus on changing individual leader behavior. Yet others focus on building a self-sustaining culture that reinforces and guides those behaviors. You will see too that building an engaged workforce is about more than just doing right by people; it requires attention to very specific issues that simultaneously contribute to employee well-being and productivity.

The Remainder of the Book

The remainder of this book is presented in six chapters that carry you from concept to practical application. In Chapter 2, we'll take a deep dive into the meaning of engagement and how engagement differs significantly from other important yet related concepts like satisfaction and commitment. We will define engagement in precise terms and position strategic employee engagement as the critical vehicle for success. To do so, we will explain how engagement ideally is described as a mapping of firm strategy to employee behavior, with both individuals and groups as a frame of reference.

In Chapter 3, we discuss what it means to create a culture of engagement. There, we will describe how many important characteristics of the work environment, including trust, justice, and fairness, relate to engagement, and discuss as well the more directly observable aspects of the work environment and their relationship to engagement. We will also introduce the important individual differences that relate to both how engagement is construed and discussed in common language, and how those individual differences also determine engagement behavior.

Chapter 4 discusses how you can diagnose the current state of the organization with particular emphasis on using employee survey data as the key metric. We will show how to translate strategy into employee behaviors that can be observed and reported on through the survey data and how to write survey questions that address the four principles of engagement we have just described.

Chapter 5 shows how you can directly impact the level of employee engagement in your organization by focusing on using survey results to develop effective action plans and design interventions with impact. The discussion of interventions will be framed by the issues of capacity, motivation, and freedom to engage.

Chapter 6 discusses the "dark side" of engagement – what happens when there is an imbalance between what employees invest and the returns they receive. Specific attention will be directed toward issues of burnout and workaholism and their relationship to engagement at work.

Finally, we will close in Chapter 7 by providing an outline of a presentation deck and the talking points you can use to introduce the concept of engagement in your organization. You will then be ready to start down the path of gaining competitive advantage for your organization through your engaged human capital. Best of luck!

Chapter 2

The "Feel and Look" of Employee Engagement

So what exactly do engaged employees feel and do that other employees do not? In the previous chapter we established the general groundwork for what engagement is, why it is important, and what needs to be done to create the conditions for it. Our focus in this chapter is a more precise definition of engagement, specifically how it feels to be engaged and what behaviors result from these feelings. Our experience in talking with most executives and managers is that they have a rough sense of what engagement means, but that they don't necessarily understand the various facets of it and how it is different from other concepts that seem similar. That is, many executives don't use the word "engagement" – they use some other more familiar or comfortable word – satisfaction, commitment – that implies engagement. After we discuss engagement feelings and the engagement behaviors that accompany these feelings, we will present the similarities and differences between engagement and other related ideas like job satisfaction and organizational commitment.

Before we get ahead of ourselves, we will show later that gaining some precision in how we think and communicate about engagement will make it much easier to implement a business strategy focused on building an engaged workforce. In short, if you don't know what it is, it is tough to make it happen.

The Feel of Engagement

In our view, there are four important components to feeling engaged:

1 feelings of urgency;
2 feelings of being focused;
3 feelings of intensity; and
4 feelings of enthusiasm.

The combination of these four elements is what makes engagement both distinct from other related concepts and simultaneously a powerful source of fulfillment for employees and competitive advantage for companies.

Urgency

Urgency is goal-directed energy and determination; we don't just want energy but we want purposeful energy. It is what developmental psychologists call "agency" and a critical component of what some have labeled "psychological capital."[1] We choose to use the term urgency here because it fits better with the notion of a force that impels action to achieve a particular end. Thus, the energy we are describing is not undifferentiated. It is a determination to achieve a particular goal. It is best understood when we think of the kind of self-talk represented in "I have to do this" and "I am not going to be stopped."[2]

The way we think of urgency is similar to how some have described "vigor" as of "physical strength, emotional energy, and cognitive liveliness"[3] but with the added emphasis on goal attainment. Because vigor is often recognized in a context of work with the implicit assumption that a particular objective is in mind, it has been described as "mental resilience and persistence in the face of adversity on the job."[4] So, vigor or energy with reference to a specific goal or objective – urgency – is at the very core of engagement. The implication of this for how we think of engagement is clear: The feeling of engagement cannot occur without a specific purpose or objective. In this sense engagement sounds much like "motivation."

The concept of urgency is central to other psychological states that are particularly relevant to the kinds of behaviors that fall within our meaning of engagement. So, goal-directed determination – urgency – is conceptually linked with resiliency, or the capacity to bounce back from temporary setbacks. It is also linked with confidence, which includes the belief that one is in fact capable of achieving a particular goal. We will have more to say about these important linkages later in this chapter.

Focus

Engaged employees feel focused on their work. Under normal circumstances, they feel zeroed in on what they are doing and aren't easily distracted by outside thoughts, or for that matter by things that aren't important to what's at hand. In a simple way, we can think of distractions at work as anything that diverts a person's attention and energy away from that which is important. So, distractions can include the typical social interactions that are in continual play in a work setting (e.g., chatting at the water cooler, discussing where to eat lunch). It can also be other thoughts: the streaming stock quotes, the nasty weather outside, and so on.

Most of us have had the experience of being occupied for extended periods of time, deeply immersed in the task at hand. We say that carefully because focus can imply behavior and we are discussing here the psychological piece of focus – being focused means having our attention and cognitive capacity tuned into "the doing" of an activity. It is not "the doing" that dominates, but the feeling of being focused on "the doing" that matters. When our attention is aimed at a single task or series of related tasks, this focus is similar to what has been described as "being in the flow."[5] Of course the nature of many jobs requires employees' attention to shift from one task or project to another based on the latest development or change in priorities. What characterizes the engaged employee, however, is that their focus is *consistently* directed at their work, and in particular, at their immediate task.

Another common way of expressing this consistent focus is to think of being "absorbed" in one's work. That experience includes a lost sense of time or the feeling that time has elapsed quickly. In addition, employees who are absorbed in their work may be more likely to have difficulty removing or detaching themselves from their work than remaining focused on their work.[6]

In many jobs there are times when an employee has little or no choice but to be focused consistently on the task at hand and where a high degree of vigilance is necessary. This would be true, for example, when distraction poses significant personal risk to oneself or others, as is the case with air traffic controllers or nuclear reactor inspectors. These are situations where vigilance is an embedded feature of the job. There is little discretion involved in such jobs. Here, we would expect the job context to be highly engineered. So, the air traffic controller and the nuclear reactor inspector work in a protected and insular environment.

Focus has a very different meaning in an environment where the employee chooses what to work on and for the duration of his or her attention span. In the extreme end of unfocused activity, we can easily think of the employee who lets his or her mind wander. That happens to all of us in varying degrees. Some examples of what we mean by focus would include:

- working on a presentation deck for an upcoming meeting without being distracted by the continual chatter on IM or email;
- listening attentively to a conversation in a weekly team meeting; or
- continually directing attention to product quality while "running" an automated machining process.

Each of these is simple to do for a brief duration. Engagement implies maintaining that focus over a more extended period; it equates to a sense of concentration and immersion in work and connotes a relative but not necessarily complete isolation from less important tasks. Thus, when the consequences of temporarily being distracted from a particular task at work are not severe, the meaning of focus becomes more salient from the organizational perspective.

Intensity

Focus alone cannot capture all of what we mean by the feelings of being engaged. For example, the reason we are startled when interrupted during a period of concentration is because of the intensity of our focus. Intensity complements focus in that it conveys the *depth* of concentration. This is driven in part by the nature of the demands of the work and the employee's skill level. When our skill level matches the demands of the task, we have to devote both our attention and energy to the task to be successful. Conversely, when our skill greatly exceeds the demands of the task we are bored and our attention and energy can go elsewhere so intensity suffers. Whereas focus implies that the portion of an employee's energy and resources that are currently being tapped are directed toward work, intensity suggests that an employee is tapping into nearly *all* available energy and resources.

In a similar vein, William Kahn, who is largely credited with introducing the concept of personal engagement at work as it is generally thought of today, explained that people are more or less "psychologically present" at different times throughout a work day.[7] By this he meant that there is a varying extent to which people bring all of their physical, cognitive, and emotional resources to their roles at work. We think this notion is similar to our use of intensity, and it also emphasizes the breadth of resources that engaged employees bring to their roles. Together, urgency, focus, and intensity suggest that, when pursuing a goal, engaged employees tap into their full breadth of resources (e.g., skills, knowledge, and energy) and apply them fully and vigorously for a significant duration.

Enthusiasm

Enthusiasm is a psychological state that simultaneously embraces both a sense of happiness and energy. It is the emotional state we refer to as "positive affect," and by its nature it connotes a strong sense of positive well-being.[8] When we think of enthusiastic employees, we conjure images of employees actively rather than passively involved. If we asked them why they are behaving as they do, they are likely to use words like "enthusiasm for what I do" and/or "I am enthusiastic about where this project is headed." When we introspect, we most often think of moments when we feel "alive" and when we do observe enthusiasm in others, we often make the attribution that they have "passion" to describe what we mean.

The experience or feeling of enthusiasm is very much at the core of what we feel when engaged in our work. This passion is not a by-product of the energy and focus but rather a defining element of the uniqueness of engagement. The sense of enthusiasm is why so many introspectively-driven definitions of engagement (which fit our common sense interpretation) refer to engagement as an emotional state. That emotional component is the positive mood state we call enthusiasm.

Importantly, while feelings of enthusiasm and passion are useful terms for describing what an engaged employee experiences, we do not intend to suggest that feelings of enthusiasm and passion are necessarily outwardly displayed by all engaged employees (although they are terms we use to describe what we think others are feeling). It is important to caution that individual and cultural differences influence the extent to which these feelings are internalized and the ways in which they might be reflected in overt behavior. That speaks to the point that what we call the "feelings" of engagement can only be accurately self-reported, a point we will discuss later in Chapter 4.

Example:
Feelings of Enthusiasm vs. Behaving Enthusiastically

One of your authors plays poker on a regular basis and saw it as his obligation as a grandfather to teach his grandchildren, regardless of gender, to play poker. He lectured on the various games of poker and then made the point that the key to being a good poker player is to maintain a poker face. He defined a poker face as one that failed to reveal how good or bad the cards in one's hand actually were. The first hand his granddaughter ever played she won the pot and her first comment was "I had great cards Poppy but I kept my poker face" – and she did. The difference between being enthusiastic about the hand one is dealt and the outward behavior that may or may not reveal the internal enthusiasm is clear.

Cross-Cultural Issues in Describing the Feelings of Engagement

An important question we often hear is whether the meaning of engagement is consistent across cultures, and more specifically whether engagement might be viewed more apprehensively in some cultures. After all, if employee engagement is something that companies are encouraging and expecting their leaders to create the conditions for in their workforce, it's important to ensure that it is viewed positively not only in all cultures in which the company does business, but also in the cultures represented by their employees.

Where we have the biggest concern is around the notion of enthusiasm. This term is often used to describe those who display their energy outwardly. These individuals may be more vocal, or simply speak with more volume – some describe people who fit this description as the "rah rah" type. This outward display of feelings of engagement is not valued in all cultures. In some Asia-Pacific cultures in particular, demonstrating control of one's emotions is valued, whereas outwardly displaying feelings of engagement is not.[9]

However, an individual can feel intensity and enthusiasm without projecting these emotions outwardly. Here are some recommendations to help companies ensure that their discussions of engagement don't create resistance in particular parts of the world or from particular demographic segments of their workforce:

- Don't use the term engagement or engaged to describe an individual in performance management discussions, unless substantiated by specific behavioral examples (e.g., not proactively addressing problems, failure to take ownership of a project, resistance to learning a new process). If employees are described as not being engaged, without the supporting behavioral examples, many will interpret this as a personality judgment or a manufactured reason to view someone negatively in the absence of any significant and documented performance problem.
- Avoid the use of terms like enthusiastic and intense in performance evaluations, leadership assessments or other HR programs. This can create the impression that there is one leadership prototype to which everyone must aspire, which can hamper efforts to build an inclusive culture and diverse leadership team.
- Recognize that the drivers of engagement may not be uniform across the workforce, and therefore efforts to increase engagement levels that center on a single corporate initiative may achieve limited success within some segments of the workforce. Consider the possibility that in some cultures creating a connection to the company's mission may be most critical, whereas in other cultures designing jobs that fully use one's skills and provide challenge may have the most impact.

- Choose wording carefully in corporate communications about employee engagement. Ensure that the stories that are told about engaged employees, and the behavioral examples of engagement that are shared, are not inconsistent with important values to cultures represented in the workforce. Having HR professionals from

---

Good to Know:
Feeling Engaged: Some or All of the Time?

Feeling engaged is a phenomenon that takes place in time but the time frame is open as one can feel momentarily engaged or typically engaged or always engaged. How we describe it in conversation and the precision with which we characterize it varies depending on whether we think of it in a very immediate sense – performing a specific task – or as an aggregate of many experiences over a considerable length of time which might be weeks, months, or even longer.

In conversation with colleagues and clients, we often describe the feeling of engagement in the following way:

> It's that kind of feeling you have at the end of a day when you ask yourself "where did the time go?" The day was a challenge but you feel good about what you did. During the day, you didn't stop and ask yourself or even think about that feeling ... you simply recognized it at the end of the day. Despite the challenge you don't feel drained; quite to the contrary, you feel both more energized and capable. It's that kind of feeling you wish you could have every day.

Our example frames the experience of engagement in the context of a single day. But we often speak about engagement in a way not restricted to a specific time period. Rather, we mentally aggregate our reflections and observations over days and weeks. So, when we ask people about being engaged we don't often focus on one experience, but the summary or aggregate of those experiences.

This distinction might seem overly nuanced. However, it becomes very relevant when we think about the kinds of organizational or personal interventions we might consider as a means of enhancing workforce engagement. In short, we do not want our employees to be momentarily engaged but we want them to be typically, usually, or always engaged in their work and task performance. As we will see later, the issue of "always engaged" can have negative consequences; companies need to be aware of the need to provide for opportunities to recover from being "always" engaged at work, perhaps through the creation of effective programs to help employees maintain good work-life balance.

different parts of the globe, and of different ethnicities, review this type of communication before it is released is a best practice.

Summary: The Feel of Engagement

Engagement is the aggregate energized feeling one has about one's work that emerges as a product of the feelings of urgency, focus, intensity, and enthusiasm. Furthermore, the engaged employee feels not only energized but competent, and this sense of competence emerges from both his own experiences and the conditions of work provided for him by his company. We presume that the feeling of engagement results in behavior that others would characterize as being engaged and it is that behavior to which we next turn.

The Look of Engagement: Employee Behavior

Having discussed what it means to feel engaged, we now turn to a discussion of the behaviors that engaged employees display that have a positive impact on organizational success. To be certain we are clear when we speak to this facet of engagement, we will specifically use the term *engagement behavior*. Of course, there are determinants of employees' engagement behavior other than their feelings of engagement. These include personality, skill levels, the personality and leadership style of their manager, the national culture in which they work, and many others. But regardless of these factors, the more engaged an employee feels, the more likely she is to demonstrate the engagement behaviors we discuss in this section.

It is now commonplace to hear arguments from consultants, executives, and HR professionals that feelings of engagement lead to employees exerting more energy and effort in their jobs, and we agree with this. Unfortunately, we hear far less about what engagement looks like in the form of behaviors. That is, we do not have a good vocabulary for capturing how engaged employees actually approach their work, and what it looks like in the eyes of others in the organization and customers or other stakeholders outside the organization. In this section we first define the components that characterize behavioral engagement and then discuss the impact of engagement behavior on *how much* work gets done, *how* work get done, and *what* work gets done. Specifically, engaged employees:

- behave in more *persistent* ways;
- respond *proactively* to emerging threats and challenges;
- *expand their roles* at work; and
- *adapt* more readily to change.

Their behavior looks different from what is typically observed and expected – and the difference can be seen not only in an individual who distinguishes him- or herself in these ways, but in an entire workforce. What we strive for is an engaged workforce, not just an engaged employee.

Persistence

Perhaps the most obvious behavioral display of engagement concerns the persistence displayed with regard to task accomplishment. We think of effort as an equivalent term but we like persistence better because it connotes effort over time. The most straightforward examples of this are employees working harder, for longer stretches of time without a break, and for longer hours during the day or week. Specific examples may include an insurance agent skipping lunch to continue investigating a customer complaint regarding the processing of a claim, or a quality assurance specialist working over the weekend to perform some product safety tests that go beyond standards.

But simply doing more of what a job requires or spending more time at it is only a piece of what engagement behavior is all about. Persistence can also take the form of increased perseverance in the face of adversity and greater resilience when a setback occurs.[10] For example, imagine a chemist at a pharmaceutical company who experiences multiple failed attempts to develop a drug formula. Perhaps a high level of engagement translates into her choice to make a third or fourth attempt rather than to concede defeat and seek out her next project.

As we suggested earlier, persistence flows from the goal-directed determination that we defined as urgency. Perhaps less immediately evident, we can expect persistent behavior when employees are enthusiastic because they believe that they can make a positive impact on the company's success. Persistence also follows when people focus so intensely that they recognize alternative paths to reaching their goal when their efforts are thwarted. The benefits of persistence to an employer are quite obvious and include the higher quality of work that results from persistence in attention to details, faster production of goods or services, and perhaps fewer employees needed and, therefore, lower labor costs.

Proactivity

A critical characteristic of engaged employees is that they are proactive rather than reactive or, even worse, passive. In its simplest form, to be proactive means taking action when the need for the action first becomes apparent to the individual, such as performing maintenance on a machine in a plant at the first sign of decreased efficiency, rather than waiting for the supervisor to authorize maintenance. It may also mean immediately doing a task for which the team as a whole is responsible, rather than waiting for the task to be assigned by the boss. In a customer service environment, a proactive employee might alert a customer to the fact that they can save money by purchasing bundled services rather than buying a variety of services or features a la carte, so that the customer doesn't discover this missed opportunity at a later time and become frustrated.

Example:
Proactive Customer-Oriented Behaviors in Call Centers

Psychologist Anat Rafaeli and her colleagues, Lital Ziklik and Lorna Doucet, have shown the considerable variety of behaviors that produce customer satisfaction that call center employees can display towards customers. In a very creative effort, they analyzed recorded calls of employees and asked the following question: What are the different categories of behaviors call center employees display to customers that might be called customer-oriented behaviors? The answer is the following kinds of behaviors:

- anticipating customer requests;
- offering explanations/justifications for decisions and actions;
- educating the customer with information they might not otherwise have;
- providing emotional support when customers are anguished; and
- offering opportunities to customers to enhance their benefits from the company.

The more an employee does these things, the more the customers say the service quality is high as a result of the call. There are tangible examples of each of these in their article.[11] Most or all of these kinds of behaviors represent examples of being proactive in serving customers.

As discussed earlier, engaged employees not only take action immediately after a need becomes evident, but they are also more likely to *recognize* or *anticipate* the need or opportunity for action in the first place. While the choice of whether to take action is likely largely influenced by motivation, recognizing the opportunity to take action is an example of how engaged employees approach their work in a qualitatively different and important way. In other words, engaged employees have a heightened sense of awareness and vigilance. They consistently have their "guard up" and are proactively looking out for the best interest of their team, the company, and its customers. Engaged employees may be more likely to take pre-emptive action to "stop the line" when a condition poses a safety risk, or to argue their point of view when faced with initial opposition. Proactivity therefore implies that employees initiate change rather than being reactive and viewing this as "management's responsibility."

This notion of employees initiating change is consistent with work psychologists Michael Frese and Doris Fay's perspective on the concept of personal initiative.[12] They argued that initiative is an overlooked concept in organizational behavior, and astutely observed that traditional views of job performance in organizational psychology imply that the tasks, processes, and work environment are dictated to the employee. For example, in traditional views, employees are selected and placed in a job where the required tasks and processes are defined, then trained to perform these tasks in particular ways, and more generally, socialized into an organizational culture. Like Frese and Fay, we strongly believe that changes in the nature of work have increased the importance of having employees who exert influence over their work environment and decisions about how their work is performed, what new products should be developed, and so forth. Today's rate of change and innovation is far too great for a company to be a market leader by relying on senior management to bear all of the responsibility for identifying and initiating change, especially where the performance of everyday tasks and processes are concerned. This is a much more positive view of employees than has existed in the past where employees have been viewed as waiting for direction and uninterested in working. Engaged employees are proactive, and they are proactive because the right kinds of conditions have been created for them to be so – we will have more to say about these conditions in Chapter 3.

The link between feeling engaged and demonstrating proactive behavior is quite clear. First, we would expect an employee who has a sense of urgency and is highly focused on her work to be more proactive than someone who is "going through the motions." Engaged employees take the initiative to avoid or prevent a problem, rather than waiting to be directed to do so. Second, engaged employees use more of their emotional and cognitive resources on the job, and for that reason are more likely to recognize a potential problem, and the need or opportunity to take action. Finally, employees who feel enthusiastic about how their own performance influences the success of the company and who internalize group and company goals are much more likely to detect barriers to goal attainment. Not only are engaged employees more likely to detect problems or opportunities in general, but this tendency is strongest for those problems or opportunities that are most central to the goals and strategic imperatives of the company.

Clearly there are many advantages to those companies whose employees demonstrate proactive behavior. Several significant advantages that haven't already been mentioned include:

- More time can be spent executing core work tasks instead of doing re-work and fire-fighting.
- Innovative opportunities are more likely to be recognized, communicated, and pursued. In some cases "taking action" simply means bringing a concern or idea forward to management, which translates into greater management awareness and ability to change quickly.
- The management burden is lessened. To the extent that lower- and mid-level employees watch out for, prevent, identify, communicate, and fix problems, management is able to spend more of their time on forward-looking, strategic activities.

Role Expansion

Engaged employees tend to see their roles in a more expansive and encompassing way. At times this can be simple and ordinary, such as helping a busy co-worker complete a task or fixing a mistake someone else made. This type of behavior is frequently seen, even if in varying degrees, but nonetheless involves temporarily stepping outside of one's role specifically to help others and more generally to help the business.

At other times, role expansion involves assuming longer-term or even permanent changes to one's role. At times a manager may delegate an increasing level of responsibility or breadth of tasks to an employee as this employee's competence becomes more apparent, or as the demands on the team change. The important characteristic here is the willingness to accept a different definition of one's role. That definition may result from the initiative of management or may be self-initiated. Sometimes responsibilities emerge that previously did not exist, as the result of a process change, the development of a new product, or a changing external environment. Other times unassigned responsibilities appear because a departing or promoted employee is not replaced or is replaced by someone who has a different skill set.

There are several reasons engaged employees are more likely to be receptive to or to initiate an expanded role. First, employee-initiated role expansion is an example of proactive behavior, and as discussed earlier, engaged employees have an inclination to act, and are less likely to wait for someone else to assume an unassigned responsibility. Next, because goal-directed employees are more likely to seek out alternative ways of meeting those goals, they also are more likely to view their roles more broadly. On the other hand, those who are less engaged are more likely to protect their existing role boundaries, as a way to stay in their comfort zone, or to avoid the pressure and increased work load that can come with additional responsibility. These employees can be heard responding to requests with "that's not my job." Finally, those employees with higher levels of self-confidence who are also engaged psychologically are more willing to expand their roles.

Role expansion too has many positive consequences for organizations, including a more flexible workforce. In some cases this might be evident in an employee temporarily doing work that typically falls within the role of a co-worker who is in the midst of a work load spike. In other cases this could mean that an employee assumes responsibility for a completely new task. This flexibility may translate directly in terms of staffing levels. Also, when employees expand their roles on their own accord, managers can spend less time identifying and assigning tasks, and give more time to other issues.

Example:
Role Expansion in a Union Environment: Yellow Roadway's Ascent to the *Most Admired*

We are, of course, arguing for the positive effects of people changing their formal assignments to be more effective. In union environments such behavior can be unacceptable due to labor–management agreements. This situation presents a paradox for unions and management with the latter wishing for increased proactivity and the former wishing to maintain existing approaches to getting the work done according to hard-won rules and regulations.

To our way of thinking, unions play a crucial role in protecting workers from potential abuses by management – that is why unions came to exist. To that end, our earlier discussion of the dangers of thinking about engagement as simply getting more out of workers is appropriate. At the same time, in an increasingly competitive world union rules preventing employees from being proactive and protective of the environment would seem not to be useful. Striking the balance between company abuse and employee proactivity would seem to be an important agenda item in future negotiations.

Yellow Roadway is a good case in point. In 1997 it was one of *Fortune Magazine*'s "Least Admired Companies" with negative earnings per share; by 2003 it was one of *Fortune Magazine*'s "Most Admired Companies" and rated number one in its industry (with earnings per share approaching $4.00 by 2004). Yellow Roadway employs 37,000 truck drivers represented by the Teamster's Union. Bill Zollars was brought to the then-Yellow in 1996 and began a campaign to turn the company into a service company that delivered goods on time with no breakage – which he pursued with vigor in 1999 when he was named CEO. Zollars accomplished his goal by working *with* the union not *against* it, treating the union as an important stakeholder along with customers. He worked with the union to permit workers to set explicit goals for on-time pick-ups and deliveries as well as for breakage, fostering proactivity on the part of employees in forging the new service image he wanted to create. Galen Monroe, a spokesman for the Teamster's Union, put the perception of Zollars this way: "We have found him to be a man of his word and whatever he says he follows through on." Long-haul trucking had never before made the kinds of promises to its customers that Zollars made – and he delivered on those promises with the help of his union employees.[13]

Adaptability

As the rate of change and innovation in today's organizations has accelerated, the value of adaptive behavior in organizations has increased. An adaptive employee will help his company anticipate and respond to changes in the competitive landscape more quickly, more successfully, and with lower costs. Adaptive employees are more likely to develop new skills as job demands change, reducing hiring needs. In addition, while many large-scale changes require formal training to facilitate skill development, adaptive employees can adjust to changes without the need for formal training, saving time and money. Adaptive employees also help minimize the extent to which management must invest time and money "championing" change efforts, which allows companies to stay ahead of their competition.

Psychologist Elaine Pulakos and her colleagues have extensively explored what adaptability is and have noted that the critical aspects of adaptability include: (a) how easily people respond to a change in their environment; and (b) how the change leads to more positive outcomes for all.[14] Some of the facets of adaptability that they include in their model are:

- solving problems creatively;
- dealing effectively with unpredictable or changing work situations;
- learning work tasks, technologies, and procedures; and
- demonstrating interpersonal adaptability.

These facets of adaptability speak to some of the ways in which engaged employees can extend themselves to meet organizational needs. Other examples of adaptive behavior include customer-facing behaviors, as when customer service representatives adapt their interpersonal style and method of providing service to fit the unique requirements of individual customers.[15] As is the case with proactive behavior, some people clearly are more predisposed to being adaptable than others. Indeed, one can think of these dimensions as representing inclinations and competencies that describe individual differences among people; we deal with those more formally in Chapters 3 and 5 in discussing issues of recruitment and selection. For our purposes here, it is more useful to think of these as representing categories of adaptive behavior. So, for example, engagement behavior in the category of Learning Work Tasks might include "taking time to search for information relevant to a newly announced software development technology that is anticipated to be the next generation of web platform programming."

Summary: The Look of Engagement

We've presented four key facets of engagement behavior that exemplify what we mean by phrases like, "She went out of her way to ensure that the project got done creatively and on time by taking on responsibilities that didn't belong to her," and/or, "It is amazing that he kept at the project even when there was one obstacle after another put in his way." So, persistence, proactivity, role expansion, and adaptability are all features of engagement behavior that, in the aggregate, connote performance above and beyond typical or normal expectations. Importantly, engagement is not just *more* performance, but performance that is persistent, adaptable, self-initiated, and/or involves taking on new responsibilities.

Strategically Aligned Engagement Behavior

As we move forward, it is important to note that we do not want to lose focus on the essential nature of engagement behaviors including adaptability, proactivity, role expansion, and persistence. But, we also want to transition from the more general to the strategic to make clear how such behaviors can uniquely create competitive advantage. This is important both for how we think and communicate about engagement within the organization.

In Chapter 1, we outlined our fourth principle of engagement: "Strategic engagement happens when people know what the organization's strategic priorities are and why, and when, the organization aligns its processes and practices – its culture – with attainment of those goals."

Thinking about strategically aligned engagement behavior requires a conversation across levels within the organization both to identify what those behaviors are and to ensure consistency or alignment across those levels so strategic goals can be accomplished. The kind of alignment and corresponding specificity we are thinking of embraces both organizational goals and the ways to achieve those goals. So, as management scholars Crott, Dickson, and Ford put it, alignment is:

> the idea of developing and making consistent the various practices, actions, policies, and procedures that managers use to communicate

to employees what is important and what is not, what has value to the organization and what does not, and what they should do and what they should not.[16]

In short, strategic alignment follows for employees when goals are shared and employees can then internalize those goals as their own. We now turn to how alignment and the process of internalization foster engagement, and along the way provide an explanation of how engagement links to the notion of employee commitment.

On Commitment, Alignment, and Internalization

We have already suggested that engagement should be distinguished from organizational commitment. One critical distinction is that commitment has many facets that reflect passive rather than active attachment, and commitment connotes attachment to the organization but not the enthusiasm, urgency, and intensity we feel characterizes the feeling associated with engagement. Of course, we think about these kinds of differences all of the time while busy executives have general ideas about what they mean and it is easy to see how the general ideas overlap. But let's get more specific about the reasons why executives see them as overlapping. One reason is because it makes simple sense to think of an engaged employee as one who understands what is required to meet organizational objectives, and by "understanding what is necessary," executives imply employees are committed to those objectives. So, executives aren't wrong when they embrace the notion of engagement in this way. They simply recognize that success is easier to attain when everyone is "on the same page;" in other words, employee behaviors are *aligned* with the organization's objectives. They see commitment (and engagement) as an alignment of individual and organizational goals and as a shared sense of "ownership" in the outcomes they are trying to create. Some may extend that thinking to the belief that if people "buy into" those goals then they would most certainly want to stay with the company and help it succeed.

Embedded in the sense of ownership we have just described is that engaged employees take on as their own the goals and mission of the larger groups to which they belong, such as the team, department,

Example:
Alignment through Employee Involvement at Boeing
The notion of alignment implies that people share a common purpose and understanding of what is essential to organizational success. That is certainly the theme at 3M as we described in the previous chapter. A similar view holds true at Boeing as described in detail in their company publication *Boeing Frontiers Online*.[17] Boeing places an emphasis on involving employees in matters that affect their own work. Boeing logic is that because what employees do is a process, involving employees in improving the processes they control is the best way to innovate. In doing so, this is seen as a way to link explicitly what employees do and how they contribute to creating value for the company.

and company. Often the term "alignment" is used to convey the notion that individuals' goals should support the attainment of team and company goals, or that teams should choose goals that contribute to the achievement of company goals. While we certainly agree with this view, we prefer a conceptualization of alignment that has a stronger intensity, one more synonymous with internalization. By internalization we mean that the goals of individuals and the organizations they work in become melded into one such that the individual sees herself as having a shared identity with the organization. For example, if you ask some people what they do, they will answer "I work for IBM" or "I work at Google." Of course, these are national "brands" but this also obviously happens with local "brands" with which employees identify. In this sense they identify what they do with where they do it; they have internalized a sense of the organization into their own identities.[18] It makes sense to assume that this kind of alignment – one that yields internalization – provides a foundation for engagement feeling and behaviors that are directed toward that which contributes to organizational success.

It is this sense of internalization and commitment to a common goal that creates the opportunity for competitive advantage. When aligned, employee energy is focused on goals that are important to the organization. Without alignment, that goal-directed energy may be directed in ways that do not benefit the company, or at least in ways that do not maximize their contributions to the company's success. We've all known employees whose time and energy is focused on those aspects of their job of most interest to them, at the expense of other aspects of their jobs that may be more critical to the success of the business. An example is the software engineer who spends long hours developing a complex product feature with little practical utility because it presents an exciting technical challenge to him (see the "20-Percent Time at Google" box for an illustration of how employee engagement helps Google avoid this problem). While the energy of this professional very well may be goal-directed and focused, that energy is nonetheless directed in a way that matches personal interests – not the goals of the organization. Therefore, the idea of alignment with team or company goals means that engaged employees are not just engaged in their day-to-day work, but in a broader sense, they are engaged in their roles with the company and its mission and values.

Example:
20-Percent Time at Google: Stretching the Boundaries?

Google is widely recognized within the business press as an innovative company. It is widely thought that this innovation is driven in part by the freedom with which engineers are allowed to pursue projects of personal interest. As the Google website proclaims, engineers are allowed what they call "20-percent time," meaning that they are "free to work on what they're really passionate about." The concept has drawn much attention and comment on various blogs. Some directly question the wisdom, some simply the practicality. The interesting point about programs like these (Genentech and 3M are other organizations with histories of promoting innovative thinking through "sponsored" time) is that they necessarily imply a high level of trust placed in employees. Very often, the topic of trust is treated in a one-sided fashion, focusing on issues related to whether employees perceive senior management as credible or trustworthy. To us, the notion of alignment that is embedded in engagement draws attention to the importance of management placing trust in employees, recognizing that they are stewards of the organization's values and are aligned with the company's strategy. When employees believe they are trusted in this way, the sense of attachment to the organization deepens, and the engagement behaviors critical to competitive advantage follow. So, the blogs that question the advantage of the 20-percent time miss the point: Engagement requires trust on the part of both employer and employee, and it is that investment – made at some risk by both parties – that creates the opportunity for high yield returns. From our perspective, Google understands that point and as a result has enjoyed the benefits.[19]

The highest levels of engagement are likely to be obtained when employees perceive that the mission of their company is congruent with their values *and* when the work itself provides for an investment of the real self in the work. Companies with effective talent management strategies know and capitalize on this to create engagement.[20] Take, for example, the "careers" page on the Johnson & Johnson website. Known for its "Credo," the values that are intended to guide everyday decision making, the company website includes quotes from some of its employees that illustrate precisely this point. One, in particular, says it perfectly:

> The Credo provides a measuring stick for every decision. For example, in the development of a new product, there are many decisions that have to be made at every step of the process, and the Credo provides consistent guidelines for such decisions. It's always reassuring to know that the Credo is a non-negotiable value system, always with you when you need it. I believe it helps us attract employees whose internal value systems are consistent with the Credo. The result is a work culture based on integrity and accountability.[21]

Harrah's Entertainment, the international entertainment company, also takes advantage of alignment in its talent management program by stressing the idea that it is hiring the right people in the first place and treating them with fairness and trust which provides the foundation on which an engaged workforce is built. Harrah's supports and requires each property manager to take responsibility not only for making wise hiring decisions but also for then following through to create an environment in which strong feelings of engagement can grow. Alignment requires both the people who will feel aligned and the environment they feel like aligning with. Later, in Chapter 5, we will speak more directly to interventions that focus on creating the kind of alignment that yields internalization of goals and the accompanying engagement feelings and behavior.

What About Employee Satisfaction?

The conversations we often have with people on the topic of engagement invariably turn to the question of what makes employee engagement different from employee satisfaction. There are both scientific and practical issues regarding the distinction. The distinction between engagement and satisfaction (and perhaps commitment as well) is an important one to the extent that it helps clarify how engagement and satisfaction each relate to important but different business outcomes.

Satisfaction has been defined as a pleasurable or positive emotional state resulting from the appraisal of one's job and job experiences.[22] Satisfaction is all about what the organization does for employees to make them feel good about being there. Thus, satisfaction conveys fulfillment of needs, satiation, and even contentment. Of importance to the discussion of engagement is what is *not* included in the meaning of satisfaction. Simply put, satisfaction doesn't capture the aspects of urgency, focus, and intensity that are central to engagement. While it may seem intuitive to expect satisfied employees also to be more motivated to perform well, the very notion of satisfaction (i.e., satiation) explicitly links it with contentment, and to maintaining the status quo. Importantly, we recognize that dissatisfaction very well may lead to considerable effort to change the situation. We also recognize that the effort to change what is unpleasant or dissatisfying may be aligned with an organizational purpose. However, the very nature of satisfaction is that it is desirable as an end-state and therefore connotes quite different forms of behavior from feelings of engagement.

Certainly we have argued that enthusiasm and the sense of well-being it connotes are part of the feelings of engagement. Also, much of the sense of satisfaction people get from the opportunity to use their skills will be most evident in situations where job demands and individual skills are closely matched, precisely one condition that contributes to feeling engaged. Nonetheless, satisfaction does not connote the sense of goal-directed energy that is essential to our conceptualization of engagement. This may be part of the reason why research has shown a relatively modest correlation between job satisfaction and job performance.[23] It may also explain why, relative to satisfaction, developing an engaged workforce is viewed by many business executives as a component of corporate strategy and a source of competitive advantage, rather than just a HR initiative to improve the quality of work life for employees.

Where Does This Take Us?

We have detailed the facets of the feelings of engagement and engagement behaviors so that readers will appreciate their multifaceted nature – and it is because they are so multifaceted that they are difficult to achieve and thus have the potential for competitive advantage. That is, not all companies can handle the multifaceted nature of engagement but those that "get it" will achieve positive consequences for people and competitive advantage for the organizations in which they work. We also clarified the distinction between the feelings of engagement and the feelings that correspond to satisfaction and other important, but different, psychological states like commitment. Here in particular, we showed that the feelings of engagement are driven by a different set of organizational conditions than those that drive satisfaction and, further, proposed that engagement leads to more productive outcomes than does satisfaction. Organizations need to decide how to both capture the persistence, proactivity, role expansion, and adaptability facets of engagement behaviors and the inclination to stay with the company associated with satisfaction as the focus of their efforts. The fact they these have different drivers does not make them different in the need for companies to pay attention to them.

Neither keeping employees nor having them behave in engaged ways is free. To satisfy employees, companies need to invest in pay and benefit plans and create security for their people. To create engagement, companies must invest in managerial and supervisor training that helps such people create and earn the trust of their people; if this came naturally everyone would do it. We are fond of saying how rare common sense is when we are told "Well, isn't it just common sense?" The Mayo Clinic interviews potential physicians for its facilities up to 20 times by different people to ensure that the people they hire have the right attitude in terms of engagement in patient care and patient satisfaction. IBM trained tens of thousands of managers to make them more sensitive to the way they treated employees and customers so that their strategy to be a consulting service firm rather than only a technology firm would be facilitated. Engagement is not free, but as we showed in Chapter 1 it can pay big dividends when we know how it feels and what it looks like – and can measure it effectively, the topic of Chapter 4.

Next we focus on the kinds of organizational cultures that can be created to foster and maintain high engagement levels in a company's workforce. To do this we have to entertain issues concerning what organizational culture is, how it results in engagement feelings and behaviors, and why that happens as it does. In a real sense we want to look inside the black box of the organizational culture–organizational performance relationship and ask what happens there and how this produces the levels of engagement we know lead to successful and competitive organizational consequences.

Chapter 3

The Key to an Engaged Workforce: An Engagement Culture

Engagement is not a one-time thing. To achieve competitive advantage, organizations must find a way to create and then sustain the level of energy and passion that people bring to work. The way to do that is by creating and sustaining a culture where engagement is not only the norm, but one which attracts the kinds of people who are disposed to doing well in that kind of environment, thereby creating a virtuous cycle of engagement behavior reinforcing and reinforced by employees. In other words, it is about putting engaged people in engaging jobs with a leadership team focused on what is necessary to enable and preserve that uniqueness.

This chapter explains:

- what organizational culture is and how it comes to be;
- how specifically to foster, maintain, and enhance a culture in which high levels of workforce engagement are likely; and
- what must also be done to foster a culture that supports the kinds of strategic engagement that are critical to achieving competitive advantage.

What is Organizational Culture?

Organizational culture is the sense people have about what their organization values, believes in, promotes, endorses, and stands for. Some organizations have a culture of innovation, others a culture of conscientiousness, others of "fire fighting" where everything gets done at the last minute, and still others have a culture of employee well-being.[1]

In fact, organizations can simultaneously have all of these as their definitions of culture. Cultures are as real a part of organizations to the people there as anything else in the organization. So, just like a company may occupy a building with 12 stories and/or be in the financial services industry, it also has a culture.

Example:
A Positive Service-Focused Culture[2]

Here is what employees say about their bank's service culture and how it feels to them:

- Service has been ingrained since we opened more than 130 years ago. That's all I've ever heard since I started working here.
- The older people here were taught customer service at the beginning and the younger people learn by watching them.
- There is no cut-throat atmosphere here like other banks. We share responsibilities and goals. People support one another – they do things they don't have to do; people aren't just looking out for themselves.
- Our branch manager sets the tone of the branch – respect, being happy, praising each other, building friendships, and getting each other lunch.

Example:
A Negative Service-Focused Culture

How the employees in another bank – a mortgage bank – describe their service culture:

- People here think about pressure, space, and hostility, not about customer service.
- Our typical approach to customers is that they are guilty until proven innocent.
- Our excessive, inflexible rules and guidelines prevent us from providing good service.
- We have a company orientation rather than a service orientation.
- No one here talks about anything, much less service.
- Management is concerned with profits, not people or service.

While there would be some differences in what people say about a company's culture, if you get to the heart of the matter about certain issues, there would be considerable agreement – like in the two different bank examples shown in the example service-focused culture boxes. These examples highlight the way employees experience these banks' cultures – one of which has a positive service culture, and the other, a negative one. The culture for service that exists within these two banks serves as a backdrop for what employees do at work and how they relate to customers. You could ask the following questions: Which bank would you rather do business with? Where would you expect higher service quality and customer satisfaction? If you answered, "In the bank with the positive service culture," the evidence overwhelmingly indicates you would be correct. So culture not only impacts its employees, but also extends well beyond organizational boundaries to impact those who have contact with the organization, for example clients/customers, suppliers, and public officials; we will have more to say about this issue of culture going beyond the boundaries of the organization later.

For now let's define culture as the way the people in an organization experience it and the meaning they attach to what they experience. "Meaning" here refers to what employees interpret as the key values and beliefs the organization has about what the organization stands for, promotes, and endorses. For present purposes, you can think of two kinds of key values and beliefs:

- How people are valued as human beings in an organization.
- What the organization values in terms of where people should be directing their energies and competencies.

The first of these relates to how organizations go about showing employees that they matter. In good times, it is relatively easy to say that "people are our most important asset." In more difficult times – when the organization is faced with making tradeoffs with scarce resources – this is far more difficult. So, these values are operative when difficult choices are made about employees in the broadest sense, such as what to do when the organization is hit severely by economic or other shocks. In perhaps more serene times, these are nonetheless still operative, but perhaps less visible and less salient. A point we will stress is that these values and how they are actually implemented – that is how we know the values – are most evident when employees feel vulnerable and at risk. Creating the right kind of culture therefore addresses our third principle of engagement: "Engagement happens when people feel safe to take action on their own initiative."

The second kind of values and beliefs concern what is promoted and endorsed regarding the specific behaviors that describe how employee energy is translated into competitive advantage. So, this may be those values and beliefs about the importance of customer service (like the examples shown earlier), innovation, operational efficiency, and the like. That is, just as there can be a positive and negative service culture, there can be positive and negative innovation and operational efficiency cultures as well. Creating the right kind of culture supports our fourth principle of engagement: "Strategic engagement happens when ... the organization aligns its ... culture ... with the attainment of [its] goals."

To summarize, organizational culture determines employee engagement at two levels: (a) that which creates and releases employee energy through the way they are treated as employees; and (b) that which channels that energy into competitive advantage through focusing on the strategic objectives of the firm be those service, innovation, and/or operational efficiency.

Creating a Culture for Engagement: How People are Valued in Organizations

The key factor leading people to experience a culture for employee engagement is the degree to which employees have trust in the organization and its management. Simply put, without trust, engagement cannot exist. Though so simply put, building and maintaining trust isn't always so simple.

The Central Role of a Culture of Trust in Employee Engagement

We all know what it means to trust someone; at least we know what this means implicitly. However, we might not all define trust in quite the same way. Trust is about how positively people feel others will

---

Example:
Living the Values at Entergy: The Foundation for Trust and Fairness

Like individuals, organizations don't get to choose their defining moment, the time in which they can choose to create a true legacy to which they and their employees can point. Katrina and the devastating aftermath that besieged New Orleans provided that opportunity for Entergy, the company that provides power to its citizens.

In the days that followed the initial storm, Entergy employees – even while addressing their own personal losses – rallied to restore the power grid supporting the city of New Orleans and surrounding affected areas. The amazing story of how Entergy employees rose to that occasion has now been documented many times over, as has the company support for those employees. Fifteen hundred employees needed to be relocated. Entergy provided access to housing, therapeutic services, child day care, and transportation. At a time of what would be heightened insecurity, employees were assured their jobs were safe, and were given time off as necessary to address personal issues and repair their own homes. In return, Entergy employees extended themselves beyond any reasonable expectation, in support of the community as well as the company.[3]

Thus, at a time when its employees were at their most vulnerable, Entergy provided what was most needed, and thereby defined by its decisions their true values. Notably, engagement wasn't part of the vocabulary or planning of Entergy leaders, although that is exactly what followed. Rather, as described by Terry Seamons, subsequently the SVP of Human Resources at Entergy, Wayne Leonard (Entergy CEO) and other executives were simply adhering to the core values they espouse.[4] What happened was the creation of a foundation for trust by ensuring employee safety and welfare at a time when employees were most vulnerable. The outcome was enhanced employee engagement and even reduced turnover. Importantly, Mr. Seamons takes care to note that sustaining engagement levels requires a constant vigilance to employee concerns. So, adhering to those core values isn't a one-time thing; credibility requires consistency and the result is trust.

---

act for them and with them in the future. When people trust others (including management), they believe that others can be counted on to protect them and work in their favor, even when they are not there to see if this in fact happens. Trust is all about believing that you can count on others to do what's right for you, regardless of whether you can even confirm that they have.[5]

Trust is always important in organizations (as it is in any relationship) but it is even more important when employees face ambiguity or uncertainty; in other words, when employees feel vulnerable. For example, in times of employment turmoil (mergers and acquisitions, high unemployment, bad public press), trust emerges even more strongly as an issue for people. Trust is what frees employees to put their full energy and commitment to work. Employees know that what they have to contribute is their time, talent, and energy. Employees want to know that when they invest these in support of their organization they are making a wise decision. In this metaphor, trust is what enables employees to make that investment. When there isn't trust, employees instead spend much of their energy protecting themselves. You might notice this in time spent seeking information about the latest rumor, or time diverted to activities that are simply not mission-related. Ask yourself the following question: In which bank described earlier are people likely to trust others and in turn, feel trusted by them? In which bank are they more likely to take the risk of being innovative and creative? In which are they more likely to feel involved and absorbed by their work? In which bank are people likely to feel engaged and be engaged?

Example:
A Culture of Trust and Implications for Employee Physical Safety: The BP Texas City Refinery

Following the catastrophic March 2005 disaster at the BP Texas City Refinery, resulting in 15 deaths and many more injuries, BP formed an independent panel to conduct a review of the company's safety culture as well as safety processes and oversight. The ensuing report[6] authored by that panel provides significant insight into the complex interrelationship of corporate structure, management, process, and culture. The Panel characterized its views on the importance of trust the following way:

> The Panel believes that a good safety culture requires a positive, trusting, and open environment with effective lines of communication between management and the workforce, including employee representatives. The single most important factor in creating a good process safety culture is trust. Employees and contractors must trust that they can report incidents, near misses, and other concerns – even when it reflects poorly on their own knowledge, skills, or conduct – without fear of punishment or repercussion.

Nurmalya Kumar, who has written extensively on trust and what he calls the "reservoir of good will," puts the issue this way:

> What really distinguishes trusting from distrusting relationships is the ability of the partner to take a leap of faith: they believe that each is interested in the other's welfare and that neither will act without first considering the action's impact on the other. … Trust … creates a reservoir of good will that helps preserve the relationship when, as will inevitably happen, one party engages in an act that its partner considers destructive.[7]

Steven Covey, author of the *Seven Habits of Highly Effective People* has the following to say about trust, distrust, and the reservoir of good will, which he terms an Emotional Bank Account:

> An Emotional Bank Account is a metaphor that describes the amount of trust that's been built up in a relationship. It's the feeling of safeness you have with another human being. If I make deposits into an Emotional Bank Account with you through courtesy, kindness, honesty, and keeping my commitments to you, I build up a reserve. When the trust account is high, communication is easy, instant, and effective.
>
> But if I have the habit of showing discourtesy, disrespect, cutting you off, overreacting, ignoring, becoming arbitrary, betraying your trust, threatening you, or playing little tin god in your life, eventually my Emotional Bank Account is overdrawn. The trust level gets very low.[8]

The metaphor is a good one because: (a) we constantly draw down our Emotional Bank Accounts just like we withdraw from our checking accounts; and (b) we know what happens when we overdraw the checking account; we have to pay big fees! We need to keep making deposits.

Notice that Covey says that the positive nature of trust is reflected in the "feeling of safeness you have with another human being." We agree with Covey and think that trust does create a feeling of safeness and the feeling of safeness it creates is the feeling that it is okay to both feel engaged and to act engaged.

Trust in Senior Leadership, Trust in Management, and Trust in the System

In our examples so far we have not distinguished between the different places where employees can put their trust. For example, employees in your organization very well may have different views about whether they trust their supervisor and whether they trust senior leadership. Further, a distinction can be made between putting trust in a person or specific persons, and the system within which people operate. So, an employee might distrust her immediate supervisor but believe that the "system" protects her interests. For example, this might be the case when performance appraisal ratings are reviewed by the local HR representative to ensure fairness. Later, in Chapter 4, we will see that well-designed employee surveys distinguish the different targets of trust.

What is often not understood is that engagement begins with the senior management team itself being engaged and trusting. This latter kind of trust comes when the CEO behaves in ways that indicate it is safe to be confrontational and open. At American Express they have an entire senior management leadership training program that focuses not only on performance excellence but also on excellence in trust and openness. Here is how Kenneth Chenault, CEO of American Express since 2001, responded in an interview with Geoff Colvin of *Fortune*:

COLVIN: [Your] culture has to include a high level of straight talk. What's your assessment of candor at American Express?

CHENAULT: I think the level is high. Is it high everywhere? That would be disingenuous to say. But one of the things I talk about often is constructive confrontation. I want to be confronted with the issues, the facts. I really want that engagement.[9]

At American Express and some other companies (e.g., General Electric, General Mills) a main goal is the development of leaders who are high on candor and high on engagement. At American Express their leadership training program is required for all people at VP and above and it is called "Leadership Inspiring Employee Engagement."

The Role of Fairness in a Culture of Engagement

The management philosopher Douglas McGregor wrote a very influential book, *The Human Side of Enterprise*,[10] in 1960 and it is as fresh and real today as it was then. The essence of his book was that the beliefs managers have about what makes their employees tick largely determine the way they behave towards them as managers. This, of course, fits well with what we have been presenting here: what leaders believe and value determines how they behave.

McGregor divided up the world's managers into two categories. One category, those who hold Theory X about employees, believes people work just for money, are basically not motivated to be creative or involved, and need to be pushed into working hard. The other managers have a different set of beliefs about people, called Theory Y. They believe that people strive to be the best they can be – that people try to self-actualize, actively participate and get involved, and love the challenge of doing a good job. The key issue for McGregor was the managerial belief system (he used the words "managerial cosmology") as the determinants of: (a) the way managers behave to employees; and (b) employee motivation and effort at work. He did not use the term engagement but you can see that he was talking precisely about the ways in which management behavior towards employees is determined by their beliefs.

Managers with a Theory Y belief system create jobs that have considerable challenge in them, offer opportunities for being innovative, provide for autonomy in task accomplishment, and offer opportunities for personal growth and development. You can see that this gets beyond the issue of trust and into the actual jobs at which people work. But McGregor was also interested in the relationships managers developed with their subordinates because he viewed people as whole people and not just as task workers. He argued that the key to a good relationship with employees was to be fair. He used terms like "get a fair break," "square shooter," and "ready to go to bat" to characterize the way employees describe a leader who is fair. And what did such fair treatment lead to? Trust – McGregor used the term "confidence."

Very interestingly, McGregor also spent time noting that fair treatment is not the only thing that leads to trust/confidence. He said that the manager being perceived to have upward influence and basic managerial competencies was also important and that the combination of these three yields confidence. As he framed it: "Confidence thus rests heavily on the subordinate's belief in the integrity of the superior"[11] with integrity being a function of fairness, upward influence, and competence.

It is very important, then, not to take away from this discussion of McGregor that all a leader has to do to have an engaged workforce is to be fair. According to McGregor he or she must also have upward influence and be competent. By upward influence he means that the immediate manager does not only take orders from above but actually influences what those orders might be and the way in which they will be carried out. In short, bosses who are seen as able to have an impact upwards are seen as bosses one can trust.

These ideas are well supported in more recent work by the management scholars James Kouzes and Barry Posner[12] who have extensively studied the issue of leader credibility. Across survey, geography, and company, they have consistently found honesty to be the leadership attribute most important to followers. Also on the top of their list are leaders who are forward-looking, inspiring, and competent. Let's turn to the issue of competence next.

The issue of competence is more difficult to summarize in a few sentences because good managers need to demonstrate competence in a number of areas. There are quite a few different competency models for leaders, with organizations often creating their own. To illustrate the point, a short list of necessary leader competencies follows:[13]

- Problem-solving skills – the ability to identify and solve new and unusual ill-defined organizational problems, including the identification of the positive and negative consequences of specific possible solutions.
- Social judgment skills – the people skills necessary to solve organizational problems in ways that mitigate conflict and acrimony as much as possible and promote positive good will necessary for the implementation of needed changes.
- Knowledge – expertise in organizing information based on knowledge resources acquired through experience and training. So,

knowledge is not just what people have in their heads, but the mental structures useful in organizing that information so that problems can be solved.

- Style – the maintenance simultaneously on influencing others to accomplish their tasks while also maintaining the social relationships necessary for that influence to have an impact. This may sound like the fairness issue in McGregor but it also emphasizes the importance of retaining a focus on task accomplishment.

In summary, effective leaders and managers have a suite of competencies to get the work done and to get it done while establishing positive personal relationships based on fair treatment. The view that they are honest and competent, combined with fair treatment by them, leads their subordinates to have trust in them. This trust then serves as the foundation for employees to feel and act engaged. The issue of fairness deserves additional attention.

Kinds of fairness Since McGregor wrote his book, we have learned a lot more about fairness. Ask someone to define fairness, and they might do so in a number of different ways. That's because there are several different types of fair treatment. One has to do with tangible rewards (money, promotions, access to training). The second kind of fairness has to do with the procedures by which decisions about rewards are made. In this type, it's not the actual rewards received that are at issue, but rather how the decision to provide or withhold a reward was made. People look at how consistently decisions are made and how predictable and uniform they are when deciding whether the decisions are procedurally fair. For example, research shows that people who are given the same sentence in a court of law can feel more or less fairly treated as a function of the procedures used in carrying out the trial or the procedures used in making an arrest in the first place.[14] Finally, there is interpersonal fairness and this has to do with whether bosses and coworkers display courtesy, warmth, and support in their interactions with us.

Note that perceptions of fairness often stem from highly visible public actions. As such, fairness can take on added weight in making judgments about the culture that exists in an organization. For example, when people hear about huge raises for some people they feel did not deserve them on equity grounds, then "confidence" and "trust" can be damaged. Incidentally, this is a good reason to have salary and bonus decisions in a company public – not just the actual raise or bonus but the procedures used to arrive at what they are. The rule is that there are no pay secrets in organizations so the amount of the pay and the bases for the decisions should be made public to prevent rumors (see the box on performance appraisals). Research from as long ago as the 1960s and 1970s in fact shows that people reliably *over*-estimate the raises given to others when pay is not public![15]

Good to Know:
The Perceived Fairness of Performance Appraisals[16]

Performance appraisals are procedures used as a basis for the distribution of rewards to workers. Research shows that five critical procedural issues predict whether people believe their performance appraisals had been fairly done:

1 The opportunity to express their feelings about the appraisal exists.
2 The existence of a formal (as compared to informal) performance appraisal program.
3 The perception that the supervisor doing the appraisal understood and had knowledge of the person's performance.
4 The presence of action plans (e.g., training) to improve performance weaknesses.
5 The frequency of the appraisals, with more frequently being perceived as more fair.

Bases for judgments of "fair" or "not fair" In addition to different kinds of activities (outcomes, procedures, interpersonal) that make up a decision about fairness, there are different standards against which these activities are judged. Everyone has heard of equity as a basis for fairness – do people get what they have earned by their efforts and performance. This is what people refer to when they say "my raise was not fair compared to Jim's." They are saying that their efforts and contributions relative to the raise they got was "unfair" compared to what Jim got given his efforts and contributions.

Another basis for making a judgment of fairness is one based on "need;" did I get what I need? Need is a frequently used basis for fairness judgments in society especially when it comes to children, the disabled, and various racial and ethnic minorities. So, people who are perceived to be in more "need" use this as a basis for judgments of fairness. Finally, there is the issue of "equality" as a basis for fairness judgments: Did I get the same as he got? Here, what is equitable and what was needed is not the issue; the issue is was I treated the same regardless. Equality is a foundation of the American culture but so are equity and need. Failure to consider each of these bases for fairness is dangerous because fairness perceptions lie at the root of trust and trust lies at the foundation for engagement. We will have considerably more to say about fairness in later chapters because it is so central as a foundation for employee engagement to exist.

Example:
Fairness at The Container Store

Fairness is not simple and straightforward; it demands sets of considerations about what is appropriate for specific people and for the good of the organization. Len Berry tells the following story about how The Container Store treated an employee fairly and achieved both personal and organizational goals:[17]

The Container Store pays based on an employee's contribution to the success of a store rather than on the position the employee occupies. This permits employees in non-management positions to earn as much as those in management positions. Fernando Ramos was in a manager position for three years and had been promoted to it from a sales position. Ramos did not enjoy the work of a manager and wanted to be more on the floor selling. So a new position for selling and training was created for him. "I go to all of the store openings to show the new people how to generate excitement on the sales floor," explains Ramos. "I hate to be behind a desk. My deal is working the floor. My salary hasn't changed; why worry?"

Culture Emergence

The culture that defines the way an organization functions, especially the way it functions *vis-à-vis* fairness and trust for the people there, does not emerge full-blown. Rather, culture evolves over time due at first primarily to the personality and values of the organization's founder. The founder imprints his or her personality and values in all of the decisions that must be made to get a start-up going. Over time, this culture is then reinforced by the leaders who follow.

Think of the start-up of an organization as a giant inkblot and it is this inkblot on which founders enact their personality. That is, the founding of an organization is actually a relatively ambiguous stimulus, just like an inkblot, and instead of saying what they see in the inkblot, founders *behave* in ways that reflect their personalities and values.

Noted MIT professor Edgar Schein in his book on *Organizational Culture and Leadership* notes that there are specific ways in which founders create the culture of their organizations followed by a number of accompanying decisions that reinforce what the culture is.[18] For example, the following actions communicate to employees what the culture is:

- what leaders pay attention to, monitor and measure;
- on what bases leaders decide to allocate resources;
- the kinds of behaviors leaders model for others; and
- the bases on which leaders recruit, select, develop, and fire people.

And some of the mechanisms that make these issues real for people are:

- the way the organization is designed and structured;
- the rituals and rites that characterize the organization;
- the myths and stories about people and events that people tell and retell; and
- the focus of the systems and procedures that are put in place.

What you see emerging here is the idea that the way the founder acts and the mechanisms and procedures he or she puts in place to manage the firm largely determine the sense people will gather about what the organization stands for and values; it also gives them a sense of where they should focus their energies and competencies. From the standpoint of employee engagement, to create a culture in which employees are engaged founders must:

- Pay attention to, monitor, and measure the way the organization values or devalues its human capital. Such organizations attend to the human component of the organization in ways that reveal concern – the organization provides for basic human issues like health care and dependent care (child, parent), encourages and supports loyalty to retain employees, and in other ways demonstrates to employees that they are more than a commodity to be hired and fired at will.
- Allocate resources in ways that facilitate employees feeling and getting engaged: the design of jobs makes use of important skills and abilities; training is offered that promotes success on the job; specific and difficult/challenging goals are set for people and they receive positive feedback on their accomplishments.
- Founders model the key behavior that underlies trust and engagement – they treat others fairly. To summarize what Covey said, what leads to trust is "Fair treatment by management."
- The systems and procedures put into place: (a) are done so in consultation with those who will be affected by them; and (b) will be fair in the way they treat employees.

And what about the mechanisms that will support this culture of engagement once created?

- The organization is designed to be relatively flat with regard to status hierarchies so that people can feel involved and committed to what happens in the organization; they are empowered to take action and feel as though what they do contributes to the organization's success.
- The rituals and rites of the organization promote involvement, celebrations of accomplishment, encouragement of risk-taking and innovation – no good deed goes unrecognized.
- People are encouraged to talk about the way their work affects them and how belonging to the organization is important to them and the things they do to promote the organization and its people – and customers, too. One popularly shared story about Nordstrom is that of a customer who came in for a Timex watch and knew precisely what they wanted but Nordstrom does not sell Timex so the sales clerk went next door and bought one and sold it to the cus-

tomer! Stories like this reveal engagement and paint a clear portrait of the way the organization functions. Whether true in the specific instance or not, the stories themselves emerge because that perspective of the culture is so widely shared.

- Organizations that want engaged employees with regard to specific outcomes – safety, service, innovation – must focus their systems and procedures in ways that promote accomplishment of those outcomes. We've worked in many organizations that claim they are service organizations but when we ask employees what the focus of the organization is, we have heard as we presented earlier variations on the following: "We don't talk about anything with management, much less service."

To maintain a culture requires not only the initial actions and reinforcement of founders but also requires continual reinforcement as the organization grows and develops. Without this, the culture can be weakened, and over time, it becomes unclear to its members. The leaders/CEOs who follow the founder must maintain and further the culture much the way that the founder created it – and they do this by what they pay attention to when they make decisions and how they implement those decisions.

Good to Know:
Posters and Coffee Mugs Do NOT Create a Culture

Many organizations think they are creating a culture by their pronouncements, posters, and coffee mugs. They may even have slogans and formal statements of organizational beliefs and values. These slogans and coffee mug captions can become fodder for jokes when they don't match the company's culture. That's because culture isn't what is written in a slogan, but it is what happens, what really happens in organizations and what people see happening to them and around them. What people see happening gets discussed and interpreted for meaning. The stories people tell become the myths that characterize the organization's culture and get shared with newcomers.

Learning the Culture

Just like organizations grow and develop their cultures over time, newcomers to organizations develop their impressions of their organization's culture over time. This happens through all of the formal and informal contacts they have with people in the organization. And for those who interact with people outside of the organization – with clients, public officials, agents for other companies – they learn from them too. All too often, companies tend to think that the culture is spread by formal means only (e.g., official contacts with management and with job training), but it is really the informal interactions at the water cooler, over lunch, at softball games and by working in the kinds of teams that characterize many work settings that the culture is "picked up."

What is really interesting about this "picking up" of the culture is that people act just like anthropologists – they diagnose what is happening in their new organization and then use the information they gather to make inferences about what the organization stands for, what it values, and the kinds of beliefs and norms that are appropriate there.[19] Once they reach some tentative conclusions about what is appropriate,

---

Example:
Socialization at Disney Theme Parks[20]

Prospective new employees at their first meetings with a Disney representative get a "realistic job preview" of what it would be like working at Disney: That they will be members of a "cast;" that they will always be on stage; and that their responsibility is to provide guests with entertainment and pleasure.

Once hired they go through two lengthy orientation phases to introduce new employees to the mission and values of Disney: (a) introduction to every aspect of the park regardless of their specific job so everyone learns about all areas and the specific care each requires; and (b) division training where cast members learn their specific roles as well as the overall philosophy of their division and its policies and procedures. Training facilities are first class with the most up-to-date audio-visual media and after training is completed there is an automatic 30-day follow-up for everyone to ensure they grasp the customer focus of Disney.

As part of employment, Disney organizes social gatherings, softball games, awards ceremonies, and so forth to solidify the acquisition of the culture.

they test these conclusions out; that is, they do not immediately trust their own conclusions because that could get them in trouble.

For example, with regard to engagement feelings and behaviors, newcomers reach a conclusion about how safe it is to feel engaged, behave in engaged ways, and try out being engaged. If the feedback and recognition they receive for being engaged is positive, then they may continue behaving that way, which is what we want. However, they are unlikely to do so if the feedback they receive is negative.

One of the earliest pieces of research on what has come to be called organizational behavior was done at the Hawthorne plant of Western Electric back in the 1940s.[21] Western Electric at the time was the production plant for the Bell telephone company making telephones and switchboards with all of the wiring those required. The researchers noticed that newcomers who came to the plant all enthusiastic and ready to put in a hard day's work after a few days looked depressed and downtrodden and the researchers wondered why this was so. What they discovered is that the newcomers who worked very hard and were very productive were literally beaten up ("binged") by the old-timers because they were seen as "rate-busters." In short, this was not an environment in which being engaged was safe.

This phenomenon of attacking engaged behavior is as true today as it was during the famous Hawthorne studies. For example, today there is a form of engagement behavior we call Organizational Citizenship Behavior or OCB.[22] OCBs are behaviors that serve the purposes of the organization and may not even be written down as formal expectations by the organization for workers. These include behaviors like helping out co-workers who are struggling, not taking more time than is necessary to clean up the work area at the end of the day, and defending the organization when it is verbally attacked. But in some organizations co-workers see such behavior as "brown-nosing" or "sucking up to management." In these organizations being engaged is not safe.

As the Hawthorne studies demonstrated, peer relationships within the work team can decidedly impact engagement levels by defining or reinforcing what is safe. However, the most important point to take away from the issue of socialization and situations being found to be unsafe is that employees apparently feel safe as a function of the way they feel treated early on by their immediate supervisors.

Thus, research shows that turnover in organizations is an early occurrence in workers' tenure and our own data at Valtera reveal that supervisors are the single most important reported reason in exit surveys for why people leave a company.

So, what does this suggest about how you on-board new workers? First, it's important to recognize that their views of the organization are formed quite early, and once formed, can be difficult to modify. Formal on-boarding programs can help to set the stage for a more engaged workforce. Orientation programs should focus on the company mission and values as part of their content to ensure that this critical information is consistently delivered to all new employees. Ideally, the mission and values of the firm will come to life in these sessions as employees hear senior leaders tell the company myths and legends that reinforce key values. These messages, of course, should then be reinforced by one's manager and colleagues. What is important to know is that it is when employees are new to the organization that they actively look for cues that tell them about what is expected (see the "Good to Know" box on psychological contracts).[23] We'll have more to say on the importance of on-boarding for values fit later.

Good to Know:
The Psychological Contract

Carnegie Mellon management scholar Denise Rousseau has done extensive writing about the idea that we have psychological (implicit) contracts with our employers and that violations of those contracts lead to negative consequences; we would say the violations lead to distrust.

She proposed that the same people who imply certain promises by their behavior turn out to frequently be those who violate the implicit promise (contract):[24]

Recruiters who over-promise, managers who say one thing and do another, co-workers who fail to provide support, and top management who send mixed messages about what is important all yield violations and subtractions from the Emotional Bank Account necessary for engagement.

Note that each agent of the psychological contract is a source of socialization to the setting – and also a potential source of distrust in the setting.

Managers should be trained on the importance of the on-boarding process and their critical role in supporting it. At a simple level, they need to ensure that the mundane issues are handled for newcomers, like having an appropriate workspace, the tools and equipment necessary to do the work, introductions to fellow workers, and so forth. However, their role needs to include far more than these. They need to ensure that people get the appropriate training needed so they can contribute to their fullest potential. They need to be careful to give them meaningful work from the beginning, provide them with specific and challenging goals (appropriate for their newcomer status though), and provide feedback along the way. They need to recognize that the promises and commitments that they make early on are critical to deliver on to help to instill a sense of trust. They also need to make some time to spend with newcomers to build a foundation for their relationship. The importance of a manager's attention to these matters is amplified when the new employee regularly telecommutes or works remotely. Additional efforts may be needed to include the new employee in after-work activities, impromptu meetings, and other events that may be unknown to the telecommuting employee.

Do the People or the Environment Make the Culture?

Readers might think that it is *only* what happens in an organization that determines the culture people there experience, but it is more than this. We noted earlier that the culture of an organization is formed early by the founder and his or her beliefs and values put into action. One of his or her influences is the kind of people attracted to, selected by, and retained by the company. Does this mean that some employees are more likely to be engaged than others? Yes, but it is more of an interaction between a person and the situation than only being due to one or the other. Recall, for example, the case of Fernando Ramos at The Container Store – he was definitely inclined to be engaged and when put in the right position, he certainly was.

Evidence for people making the culture   John Holland, the great theorist on careers, proposed that not only do people differ in their career personalities, but the environments for people in different careers will also differ. In short, Holland proposed that people who are more artistic will more likely work with others who are also artistic just as those who are more investigative will work with people who are similar to them. The fact that people similar to each other tend to occupy certain functions or even whole organizations leads the settings to have different cultures.[25]

Good to Know:
Personality and Career Interests

Holland says careers can be segmented into a hexagon with there being six different types of careers and the personalities that define them, as follows:

1 *Realistic* – Conforming, dogmatic, hardheaded, persistent, practical
2 *Investigative* – Analytical, cautious, complex, curious, intellectual, precise
3 *Artistic* – Complicated, disorderly, expressive, imaginative, intuitive
4 *Social* – Agreeable, empathic, generous, idealistic, patient, kind, warm
5 *Enterprising* – Acquisitive, ambitious, domineering, enthusiastic, forceful
6 *Conventional* – Careful, conscientious, efficient, orderly, thorough.

Holland shows you can predict the careers people will end up in with considerable accuracy based on an interest inventory and that people's career interests and personality remain very stable over a life time.

For example, let us think about an advertising firm and the kind of culture it might have and contrast it with an accounting firm's culture. According to Holland, accountants have Conventional career interests and advertising people have Artistic vocational interests. Following Holland's views, we would likely find the accounting firm characterized by people who are high on conscientiousness, behaving in ways that informally demand, support and reward conformity, dependability, and being methodical in their behavior. Contrast that with the advertising agency and Artistic types. They would be impulsive, non-conforming and expressive and the culture would be one that informally demands, supports, and rewards these types of behaviors because it is made up of those kinds of people.

What this discussion suggests is that trust and the fairness issues that support it might take on different guises as a function of the kind of career environment in which it was examined. Further, it suggests that the behavioral manifestations of engagement might differ in different career environments and for people in different functions in an organization – but that the *feelings* of engagement would not necessarily differ at all. That is, in the Enterprising and Artistic environments we are more likely to observe enthusiasm and excitement and high levels of activity whereas in the Conventional and Investigative worlds such boisterousness would not be likely. But the feelings of engagement – the feelings of involvement, absorption, and identification with the work and the organization would not be different. The moral of this story is that we need to look more deeply into people and what they accomplish to establish their level of engagement than just looking at their outward behavior.

Potential personality correlates of the engaged employee We can think about engaged employees as those who are generally more upbeat and positive about themselves and their worlds. For 50 years or more we have documented scientifically that some people are more positive than others about life and work and that this view has lots of positive consequences. For example, more positive people are more satisfied at work, less likely to be absent, more likely to work well with co-workers (and customers), and also to have fewer headaches, heart attacks, and longer-lived marriages! Can you test for the positive personality? Yes. People who are more positive are also less neurotic (they are more stable) and have what is called "positive affectivity" (they tend to see the world more positively); tests for both of these exist from reputable test publishers.

But you don't only want a positive personality because that is only part of engagement. You also want employees who are conscientious so they will persist in their work efforts. Here, too, there are good measures of conscientiousness available. In fact the research shows that conscientiousness and neuroticism are the two best personality predictors of performance in most jobs. We hypothesize that this is true because conscientious and non-neurotic people are more easily engaged and it is this engagement that yields higher levels of work

---

Example:
Creating an Engaged Workforce at Harrah's Entertainment, Inc.

We had the good fortune to speak with Nigel Martin, VP of HR at Harrah's about what they do to try to ensure their employees are engaged. In short they do two things: (a) hire people likely to be engaged in the roles and kind of business they operate in; and then (b) ensure they are surrounded with supervisors, peers, communications, and the support to be engaged.

For customer-facing roles, they seek upbeat people with a positive attitude and they assess for these characteristics formally by putting potential employees through a series of panel interviews. In one version of the hiring process, candidates meet in a room with 20 others and are asked to learn what they can in a few minutes from the person sitting to their left and then present what they learned to the rest of the group. This is all observed by trained interviewers.

With regard to surrounding people with the right kinds of peers, all new employees are sent to a 4- to 5-day entertainment-themed orientation where they meet with and interact with other new employees. Supervisors are trained to focus in on the following three issues: (a) understand your people and your team and their lives; (b) help them do their jobs well by providing them the resources they require; and (c) provide people with personalized recognition when they try to be even more effective than they have been.

Harrah's understands you must do it all to get the engagement that produces competitive advantage, and the more you put into the relationship, the more the employees and the company get back.

---

performance. So, while you can do a lot to create an engaged workforce, one critical thing that you can do begins before employees even join the organization – it's hiring those who are more likely predisposed to be engaged! For employees, this might mean adding personality measures to a selection process. But, the focus on selection should also extend to first-line managers (and other leaders) who are critical in helping to create and sustain a culture of trust and engagement. For managers, the selection or even promotion process might be extended to include:

• Behavioral interview questions that focus on fundamental issues for fostering a culture of engagement, such as how they: set goals with employees and provide feedback; ensure that direct reports understand the company direction and how they support it; provide

employees with autonomy and challenge in their jobs; ensure the respectful and fair treatment of employees; have repaired a relationship where trust has been compromised; and so on.
- Assessment center processes that include role plays and simulations that address interpersonal situations (e.g., how they coach an employee with a performance problem).
- Engagement metrics from scorecards as input into promotion decisions.

Good to Know:
The Role of Supervisor Personality in Creating a Culture of Fairness

First-line supervisors "set the tone" for the fairness employees experience at work. What personality attributes of these people predict the procedural fairness climate they create for their subordinates?

Recent research[26] shows that the first-line supervisors higher on a number of the following attributes produce fairer procedural justice climates for their employees:

1 agreeableness;
2 conscientiousness; and
3 emotional stability.

The research further showed that "extroversion" and "openness to experience" were not significant predictors.

What is really interesting about having an engaged workforce is that the word spreads about what it is like to work in the organization because employees tell their friends and family. This creates a positive cycle whereby the people attracted to an organization for employment are those who wish to be as engaged as their friends and family members are! It is for this reason that many managers with whom we have consulted think of organizational pride and low turnover as manifestations of employee engagement.

The Role of the Work Itself in a Culture of Engagement

So, you have the right kinds of positive people and the right kinds of fair management so voilà you have an engaged workforce! Well, almost. The missing element in this matrix of people and situations is the work people actually do. The work we actually do is what absorbs us, what we feel enthusiastic about and persist at, and what gives us the feeling that we are being fulfilled at work. Job design gurus Richard Hackman and Greg Oldham spoke about this kind of work as work that is high on meaningfulness – the work itself and the outcome(s) from the work are important.[27]

When the work itself is meaningful it is also said to have intrinsic motivation. This means that it is not the pay or recognition that yields positive feelings of engagement, but the work itself. In combination the following elements make work meaningful: work that people find challenging; has variety; permits them to be relatively autonomous in what they do and how they do it; and provides feedback directly as a product of doing the work. Of course, work that has these attributes would be designed for employees by founders and managers who have what McGregor called a Theory Y mentality about what motivates people so the linkage to leadership and management is a tight one. That is, the same managers who will treat people fairly and foster in them a sense of trust are also more likely to be the managers who will ensure that the work itself is meaningful.

Does this mean that assembly line work cannot be meaningful? No, but it does mean that it is more difficult for such work to be made meaningful. All work can be made more meaningful by altering characteristics of the work being done and the way it is done. For example, assembly line jobs can be made more meaningful through:

- *variety*, such that people do not always do the same task;
- *autonomy*, such that people, or even teams, have goals set for them but then determine how they will best meet these goals;
- *challenge*, by setting specific, difficult goals for people and teams that they accept;
- *feedback*: by providing continuous feedback for how well the work is being done.

In addition, any work can also be made more meaningful by helping employees to see their work in the greater context of the organization – for example, the assembly line worker in an auto plant is part of an organization that plays a vital role in the community by providing jobs, job skills training, and financial support for community events and organizations.

Good to Know:
Goal Setting and Engagement

Psychologists Edwin Locke and Gary Latham have shown over the years that the highest levels of effort and performance on the job are observed when people work at specific, difficult goals that they accept. The research clearly shows that people who are told to "do your best" do not actually do their best. People do their best when they are provided with specific, difficult goals that they accept.[28]

The research also shows that actually reaching goals creates a self-fulfilling cycle that spirals upwards to even higher levels of performance; goal accomplishment itself is rewarding.

Good to Know:
The Importance of Feedback

More than 70 years ago Morris Viteles,[29] one of the early founders of Industrial and Organizational Psychology, had this to say about the importance of feedback:

[G]roups of workers without knowledge of results tend to show a persistently lower level of performance than workers on the same task who continuously know how well they are doing. Perhaps further consideration should be given, particularly in repetitive work, to wider use of readily visible output recording devices. ... [T]he incentive would be particularly strong if the indicator registered the accumulating output in terms of ... dollars.

Our work in numerous organizations reveals that many employees receive no feedback (knowledge of results) on their direct contributions to organizational success and are thus disengaged from such success.

The Role of Monetary Incentives in a Culture of Engagement

Readers might have noticed that we have not talked about pay except when we discussed the different bases for fairness judgments by employees – i.e., we discussed pay equity issues. That's because we don't consider pay and other financial incentives (bonuses, profit sharing) as key to employee engagement. While employees may want more pay, they are unlikely to leave a job that they love in an organization that treats them well to go to an organization where they know that they won't be treated well but will get more money.

People come to work for pay but get engaged at work because the work they do is meaningful and because they work for managers who are competent, have upward influence, and are fair. They also are engaged when they work with others who are engaged, usually because of a combination of their own knowledge, skills, abilities, and other characteristics (KSAOs) and the kinds of workplace conditions that promote engagement that we outlined earlier.

People will focus their energies and competencies on achieving pay when the reward system in which they work focuses incentives on specific kinds of goal accomplishments. Thus, sales people typically have incentive-based pay, pay based on how much they sell. There is nothing inherently wrong with such incentive systems, but they can have the drawback of focusing people on the very specific behaviors necessary to get the incentives.

For example, consider insurance agents who are paid to gain new policyholders. If paid to gain new policyholders (e.g., there are higher incentives for earlier payments by policyholders) then agents will sell new policies. The problem is they will ignore old policyholders because the incentives are not there to serve them well. State Farm Insurance Company identified this problem a number of years ago and changed the incentive system to also include policyholder retention. So, incentive systems can yield the behavior of interest, policyholder retention, only if the incentive system is specifically tied to that outcome.

Salary is not a reward for anything but coming to work. An annual salary raise is almost worthless with regard to daily motivation and engagement because of the frequency with which it is given and the disconnect between specific acts and the raise. Annual increases based on profit-sharing are superior because profit-sharing, especially at the work unit or team level, involves interaction and support with and from others and that can be very engaging and make work meaningful.

Some forms of incentives and pay can thus be effective in creating engagement but they must be used very carefully or they will at best fail to achieve the goal they were designed for and at worst result in negative outcomes (like selling policies instead of retaining policyholders).

Does Organizational Success Impact Employee Engagement?

In the research we have been doing on the relationship between employee engagement and organizational performance (see Chapter 1) as well as in other research with which we are familiar, we have found that when the organization a person works for is financially successful and/or in other ways gets identified positively then employee engagement (and other employee attitudes) rise. The reverse is also true as revealed in a conversation we had with Anthony (Tony) Murphy, Senior VP of HR at Eli Lilly.[30]

Mr. Murphy told us that back in the 1990s when his company (and other pharmaceutical houses) was doing very well financially, Lilly concluded that it was important to think through ways it might repay its employees' efforts, the source of that financial success. The decision reached was to present stock options to all employees regardless of position or rank. Satisfaction and engagement rose appreciably and stayed high – and then they noticed that there was a relationship between the stock price and scores on their engagement survey. The bottom line on that relationship was that as the stock price remained high so did the level of engagement but when the stock price declined there was a noticeable decline in employee engagement.

Once they identified this trend it became clear to Mr. Murphy and his team that employees were overly focusing on the financial success of the company as an index of success so they quickly made very public the other successes Lilly was having around the world. In fact, Lilly had numerous productive and excellent successes over the years but for a variety of reasons (changes in rules governing the way they can market products, for example) those were not reflected positively in the stock price. Also not positively reflected in the stock price were awards they had won over the years nationally and internationally (in Spain and Brazil, for example) as one of the best companies to work for. So Lilly implemented a number of actions over a several year period to reinforce this broader view of success:

1 Lilly put into place a communications strategy for ensuring that employees became aware of the many positive things that the company is doing and accomplishing, including the impact of new discoveries on the quality of life for people who use the pharmaceuticals they produce.

2 Lilly implemented a new leadership training program that focused leadership not only on the rational business decisions they must make but on the emotional life of employees, including employee engagement.

3 Lilly developed communication pieces that explain the inherent delays that exist between discoveries in research and other positive changes at Lilly and changes in the company's share value. These communication pieces helped employees focus on the long-term benefits of research successes and Lilly as a place to work.

4 Lilly created a company-wide and world-wide four day forum to solicit input from all employees via the Web. The website was manned by trained senior leaders and was completely interactive. Specific topics were proposed for input but they were not at all limiting except they focused specifically on the future of the company. As an index of the behavioral engagement of Lilly employees, management was gratified to observe that fully one-half of all Lilly employees participated via the Web in this demonstration by Lilly that it wanted straight talk.

The bottom line on this discussion is that the success of a company feeds back into the engagement of the company's employees; engagement leading to success is not a one-way street. People like to see positive consequences from what they do and those positive consequences lead them to feel good about what they do and who they are and fosters engagement behaviors to produce still more positive results. The first rule we learn is that it is very important for companies to think about the ways in which success can be made apparent to employees because it is those employees who helped create the success. The second rule we learn is that it is important to focus employees on the total variety of successes the company is having because that is what creates the broad base of such successes with which they can identify.

The Role of Culture in Creating Strategic Employee Engagement

We have repeatedly emphasized the importance of trust and fairness for creating a culture for engagement. This is true regardless of whether the source of competitive advantage is service, innovation, or efficiency. That is, a culture of engagement is basic and relevant regardless of the specific focus for competitive advantage in the organization. However, we have also emphasized that another level of culture is important as well, i.e., those values and beliefs that connect to and determine how well the organization performs against specific strategic objectives. It is here that the foundation is created for determining how employee energy is channeled in a form that creates competitive advantage. In many of our illustrations and descriptions of culture, we have drawn from what is known about service organizations because those are widely experienced by many people both as employees and as customers. However, as we've noted, there are other cultures as well, such as cultures for innovation, efficiency, work quality, safety, and so on.

We detailed in Chapter 2 that thinking about strategic engagement requires that we identify the specific behaviors that reflect what is valued and what creates competitive advantage. We also indicated that to achieve alignment it is necessary that it be supported by the organization's culture. We think it obvious that the behaviors most closely aligned with a quality-oriented culture might be different than the behaviors more consistent with an innovation-oriented culture. For example, a quality-oriented culture would likely support behaviors that are consistent with reliability and standardization. Conscientious behaviors come to mind. On the other hand, behaviors aligned with a culture of innovation would likely reflect the acquisition of new knowledge, thus breaking away from current standardization. Importantly, it isn't necessary to think of these behaviors as necessarily conflicting – rather it is a matter of defining, communicating, and reinforcing those behaviors that are most critical to competitive advantage.

That is, certain kinds of behaviors, while inherently "good," do not necessarily directly contribute to competitive advantage unless they are directly focused on the strategic objectives of interest. For example, while certain kinds of behaviors, like conscientiousness, are always generally positive, we have shown elsewhere that across companies generic conscientiousness is unrelated to customer satisfaction while *customer-focused conscientiousness* is related to customer satisfaction![31]

How Culture Supports Alignment

Culture directly supports alignment because the culture provides the cues people need to guide their behavior. So, the job of guiding behavior doesn't fall on the manager as the collective direction of the team or workgroup supports those choices as well. The cues people receive are generally on what's most important (e.g., "we don't do that here"), the subjects about which people meet and talk, the emphasis on what is described in the employment interview, and the organizational lore that gets repeated and emphasized in conversation, myths, and stories.

Summary

Organizational culture is the sense people have about what their organization values, believes in, promotes, endorses, and stands for. Culture emerges from the kinds of decisions founders make early in the life of an organization. The culture they create is based primarily on what they attend to as being important and at what they allocate scarce resources. Culture is not forever; it must be maintained and enhanced. Here are the six critical features of a culture in which employee engagement is likely to exist and that yield the kind of competitive advantage we think is possible through human capital:

1 All levels of management reveal to employees that they can be trusted. They do this by treating people as valued resources and especially by treating people fairly. They treat people fairly in the ways they interact with them, in the policies and procedures they design for employees (like performance appraisal systems), and in the outcomes employees receive – like promotions and raises.
2 Trust in management, especially perhaps trust in one's immediate supervisor, is the key foundation to an engagement culture where employees can feel engaged and behave engaged. This is so because they feel safe to be proactive, to persist at difficult tasks, to be

adaptable and to take risks to do what they see needs doing even though it may not be in their formal job description. The key to trust is fairness.

3 The on-boarding process is the way people learn the culture of an organization. From the first contacts organizations have with potential employees through the early on-boarding process organizations must imbue new employees with the values and goals of the company. They do this through formal training that focuses on company values as well as the skills required to do the work, through informal opportunities for interaction, and through continual re-training. But perhaps the key to learning the culture is what people see actually happening to them and around them in the form of behavior – by co-workers and supervisors. This makes it essential that care be taken where the rubber meets the road on the front lines of work in organizations that what happens there displays the values of the company in the best light possible.

4 The actual jobs at which people work must be designed such that they require people to be the best and do their best. Such jobs are high on meaningfulness – they permit autonomy, provide a challenge, and give feedback from the work itself. Such jobs yield a sense of urgency and enthusiasm and require a sense of urgency and focus and these are the key facets of the feelings of engagement.

5 Hire carefully because you can hire people more likely to be engaged. Focus on hiring people with positive affect who are also conscientious because work performance requires both skill and motivation. Do NOT make the error of thinking that if you get the "right stuff" your job is done; the "right stuff" is "right" when they have the "right" culture in which to live.

6 Employee engagement is affected by and also has an effect on organizational success. Successful organizations, other things being equal, will have more engaged employees and vice versa; success causes engagement and engagement causes success such that a positive success cycle is created.

If we had one message to leave with readers about creating the culture required then it is this: Management at all levels, by its actions and not by its words, determines the sense people have of what the culture is and what it stands for. The more that culture promotes valuing people through trust, fairness, jobs, procedures and so forth the more likely employees are to be engaged. Further, the more the organization acts through its decisions and policies to communicate its strategic imperatives the more likely employees are to be strategically engaged.

Reflection:
Organizational Culture as Red Wine

In another place, one of us had this to say about organizational culture:[32]

> Organizational culture is like red wine – the quality is determined by what goes into it, how it is treated, and how long it ages. Founders' personalities, values and beliefs, the strategies and structures they enact, and the behaviors they reward, support, and expect determine culture. Effective cultures age well up to a point but they can turn bad; cultures must be monitored for their fit to their competitive environment.

Chapter 4

Phase 1 of Creating and Executing an Engagement Campaign: Diagnostics and the Engagement Survey

We have presented considerable detail about what an engagement culture is and how it contributes to and directs the energy that employees bring to the job. Now we turn to how to create an action plan for building and sustaining an engaged workforce. We see this as a process similar to a political "campaign" over an extended period, where there are gains and setbacks, and where all candidates have prior histories, strengths to leverage, and weaknesses to overcome. In this and the following chapter, we provide an outline that will guide your decision making. Like a political campaign, it requires continual rethinking and retooling as successes and failures create momentum along the way. It is a continual and iterative process of diagnosis and intervention. This chapter is about diagnosis, and the next chapter is about intervention. However, we briefly discuss the issues concerning intervention in this chapter so we understand where the diagnosis needs to go and why.

In Chapters 1 and 3 we gave a preview of the kinds of interventions that build an engaged workforce. Reflecting the principles of engagement we introduced in Chapter 1, here are the five questions to be answered to determine whether and why those interventions are appropriate:

1 *Does company leadership understand the leverage points for creating competitive advantage through employee engagement?* – Do leaders understand the fundamental ways in which employee engagement

contributes vitally to the organization's depth of human capital? Do leaders understand and agree upon their personal roles in facilitating employee engagement?

2 *Do employees know what the strategic focus of their engagement should be?* – Do people know how what they do matters and where it fits in the bigger picture of the organization's long-term strategic goals? Do they have goals that align their behavior with their company's goals and their own individual talents and interests?

3 *Do employees have the intellectual, social, and psychological capacity to engage?* – In present day parlance, do employees have the necessary "engagement capital?" Do they possess the energy and resiliency needed to adapt to changing conditions and persist when confronted with obstacles? Do employees have the resources and tools they need to make their investment of energy worthwhile? Do they have balance between work and personal time to maintain that level of engagement over the duration of their employment? Do they have the support networks needed to maintain engagement under duress?

4 *Do they have a reason to engage?* – Do they have a sense of identity and interest in both what they do and the purpose they serve? Does their work matter to them individually and to those around them? Do the skills they possess align with what they have to do?

5 *Do people feel safe and free to engage?* – Are the conditions in place such that employees feel free to release their energy and talent? This is a question of autonomy and empowerment.

These five questions create the framework for both the diagnostic and intervention phases of the engagement campaign. Moreover, answering these questions creates the link from the work environment to the feelings of engagement and, in turn, to the engagement behaviors that lead to competitive advantage.

Looking forward to the next chapter on interventions, our eventual aim here is to identify the kinds of organizational processes that create the conditions to support an engaged workforce. Importantly, by acknowledging the need for intervention, we are explicitly indicating that building an engaged workforce requires more than an "employee engagement survey." A well-designed survey provides data, *but it is what an organization does with the data that matters.*

Intervention implies change: Change in how work is structured and processes are organized; change in the way leaders interact with employees; and hopefully, subsequent change in engagement feelings and behaviors. That means that interventions can be targeted on both organizational processes and also directly on individual behavior.

The kinds of interventions that we have in mind require an investment. Such investments obviously carry risk, both of the direct financial kind and of the possibility of failure. The good news is that there is a body of organizational and psychological science that provides a solid foundation as to the appropriate processes and forms these interventions might take. Our suggestions for building and maintaining an engaged workforce are based on such evidence mixed with our own experience as consultants.

Because we offer our suggestions for creating an engaged workforce using an evidence-based approach, we are often asked a series of questions: "If you know what drives engagement, why do we need to do a survey? Shouldn't what drives engagement be consistent across time, people, and perhaps even cultures? Why can't we just address those issues directly?" The answers to these questions are sometimes more complex than we would like them to be for there is some truth in the implied answer to the rhetorical questions. For example, the kinds of things leaders should do to build trust and demonstrate fairness are right to do regardless of circumstance and regardless of whether a survey is ever done. Nonetheless, consider the following:

1 Well-designed and implemented survey diagnostics are an efficient approach to identifying where to direct action in a specific setting. So, it is in this context that we think of the engagement survey as efficiently leading to action planning and subsequent execution of those plans.
2 Effectively implemented diagnostics are positively intrusive. They communicate messages about what is valued within the organization. They communicate to employees how seriously management thinks about employee engagement and all that it implies. Diagnostics lead employees to think about their work and their contributions to the organization. Diagnostics give employees and their leaders feedback that confirms or denies their

own private views and can lead to a more realistic and constructive way of thinking about people, their jobs, and organizational effectiveness.

3 Not every organization starts at the same place, and the starting point determines the nature (intensity, duration, focus) of the intervention(s) that follow from the diagnostics. In one way, this is the same as saying every organization has its own history and corresponding legacy. At times, that legacy works against the goals of the engagement campaign. Further, you or some other leader may have inherited that legacy and lack the background to fully understand its implications. An appropriately designed survey can help illuminate those issues.

Diagnostics certainly can take different forms. They range from the casual observation and collection of anecdotes to the sophisticated engagement survey, which is the focus of this chapter. Indeed, our recommended strategy comprises several diagnostic activities, the engagement survey being only the most visible form.

Pre-Survey Diagnostic Activities

Our steps to implement an engagement campaign are described here as a complete framework. Many organizations will find they have already completed parts of this campaign strategy, or choose to modify the plan to fit "where they are" within the context of an ongoing process. This would certainly be the case in an organization that has already been conducting employee surveys on a regular basis, perhaps already referring to them as "engagement surveys." For the sake of completeness, our "model" campaign strategy is written from the perspective of what the organization needs to consider with the assumption that no prior activity has occurred.

Step 1: Conduct the Background Check and Acquire the "Language"

The first step in the diagnostic phase is intended to define strategic engagement "as we want it to look here." Most importantly, any lack of clarity in defining what engagement means at a strategic level, and how it is manifested in the behavior of line employees, means that further efforts to communicate with the organization as a whole will be unsuccessful.

PepsiCo expresses their understanding of this link in their 2007 annual report:

> As a guide for associates in all functions and at all levels of our orga-
> nization, we introduced the PepsiCo Leadership and Individual Effec-
> tiveness Model in 2007. By communicating what's important at
> PepsiCo and what we value from each of our associates, we are helping
> to shape an unrivaled corporate environment that provides our
> company with the ultimate competitive advantage.[1]

The internal HR Consultant will often have more direct access to information that speaks to defining how employee engagement translates into competitive advantage than will the external consultant. The external consultant will find the job more difficult as the public messaging used by companies is obviously written to respond to many legitimate agendas. Clearly, though, the more complete this definition of what strategic engagement means to the target company and in the language used there, the easier the task of both communicating and measuring strategic engagement.

When we get involved with clients, we make the point of researching publicly available documents to understand better the messaging surrounding company strategy and relevant business criteria. At times, we find that what is "mission critical" is fully articulated in the annual report. More often, we find relevant information openly presented in presentations to the financial investment world which can easily be found on corporate "investor relations" websites. Here, while words are carefully chosen, they tend to speak directly to how the company believes value is added in the marketplace. For example, innovation-driven companies will speak to the R&D pipeline of new products. Efficiency as a core value is often described in terms of "scale" or "cost control." These are the metrics financial analysts pay attention to because knowing where the company falls on the metrics relevant to the strategy of organizations gives them insight into potential future market performance. In addition, we often find that valuable information is provided within the organization's employment branding materials, with the career sections of company websites a good starting point.

The important task from a human capital perspective is to translate these explicit value statements into the specific kinds of engagement behaviors that are valued and regarded as a source of competitive advantage. At times that can require a bit of detailed follow-up. For example, a simple reading of IBM's 2007 annual report indicates that part of their strategy in addressing increasing globalization is to replace vertical hierarchies with horizontally integrated teams.[2] As part of the conversation with executives, we would naturally ask about the kinds of behaviors that reflect "success" in such teams. We aren't saying that this is where we would end with our definition of strategic engagement, but we clearly would use this as a point of departure or at least follow up in our interview. Again, at times our homework is partly done for us, such as expressed in the 2005 annual report from Tesoro Corporation, where the importance of proactive engagement behavior is articulated directly: "people continually look for new and better ways to work. By being proactive in every facet of our business ... we continue to create shareholder value."[3]

In summary, the important outcome of this step is to acquire an understanding of how engagement, performance, and strategy are discussed both directly and indirectly within the organization. By being aware of the strategy and the language used to portray that strategy *vis-à-vis* people, we are better positioned to help leaders diagnose and then improve the level of engagement of their workforce.

Step 2: Engage Leadership to Define Strategic Engagement and the Supporting Culture

We work from the premise that senior leaders both directly and indirectly influence the organization's culture, which in turn facilitates or hinders employee engagement. Therefore, it is critical to assess whether there is alignment within the senior leadership team as to the focus and purpose of the engagement effort. Some of the relevant questions include:

• Is there a common expectation for what engagement means for both the organization and its employees?

- Is there a common view of the challenges facing the team as it moves forward and the timelines for implementing the engagement campaign?
- Do all understand the role of culture and the work environment in promoting employee engagement?
- Is the role of engagement in creating competitive advantage explicitly defined?

It is difficult to obtain access to senior leadership. Often, an engagement initiative begins with a call from a senior HR professional to an external consultant – the need for an engagement survey has been defined and the HR professional is looking for a consultant or vendor to provide the relevant support. A proposal is requested, and the HR team evaluates responses to a pre-defined set of questions that may seek answers about any number of factors specific to conducting an engagement survey. Unfortunately, it is rare to see a "request for proposal" that in any way addresses the need to engage senior leadership in the process. But that is very short-sighted.

We understand that internal consultants do not always have the influence to guide corporate thinking on engagement and must rely on HR leadership to fill this role. We also of course understand that external consultants can find it difficult to obtain access to corporate leaders. But access to senior leadership must be obtained, because our experience in a large number of organizations suggests that members of the senior management team may have very different perspectives on what engagement is and why it is important.

Prior to the survey itself, there must be a diagnosis of how the organization understands employee engagement and the directions in which organizational momentum is moving. We do not see this as a survey-driven initiative at this initial stage. Rather, it is better to think of this as a sequence of conversations with the top few levels of leadership. It's best not to assume that the views within and across these levels are consistent, although they may certainly be. Also, it's best not to assume that the senior leadership team can openly discuss and resolve differences if in fact they exist. At a minimum, one outcome of this exercise is an identification of any "disconnects" that exist at the top. In the better case, an opportunity emerges to clarify and align the messages of the senior leadership team. Some questions worth asking include:

- Where are you dissatisfied with or have inconsistent views of the progress the organization is making in fulfilling your strategic plan?
- Where do you see a lack of alignment between where people spend their time and effort and where you think they should be directing their effort? Where does the disconnect occur? Why do you think that is? Towards what activities or goals does employee energy seem to go?
- What do you think will make it difficult to change this situation?
- Has it always been this way? Has there been a change in strategic focus? What has changed or is changing in the organization or marketplace that is facilitating or hindering progress?
- What would be different if employees were maximally engaged?
- How would you know your employees are maximally engaged – what do you want to see?

The organization's leader may wish to rely on internal staff (HR staff, 6 Sigma black belts) to conduct such an analysis, but at times it is better accomplished with the help of a third-party team who may more objectively capture, aggregate, and make sense of the conversations. The information collected at this stage of activity is often times quite sensitive as executives are politically attuned to "turf" issues. A trusted third party may more easily probe to gather information and to test the assumptions he or she draws from those conversations. Third parties may also experience less difficulty in sifting through the "private theories" that often emerge in these conversations and may be more likely to have the probing skills necessary to ensure they understand what they are hearing.

Through iterative feedback to the leadership team, this diagnostic phase can help to ensure that a common view emerges among the leadership team as to: (a) what the team wants to achieve through employee engagement; (b) how they think about what employee engagement is; and (c) the barriers that prevent the company from achieving its strategic plan *vis-à-vis* its people. It is also important here to identify those components of the culture that represent the fundamental values of the company that are important to celebrate and preserve. Actually, it isn't important whether "engagement" is the defining attribute of this activity. For example, it would be perfectly appropriate to frame the conversation in terms of leadership–organization–employee alignment.

This phase of activity sets the stage for how employee engagement matters within the context of the culture and strategy of the company. Most importantly, this discussion puts strategy first, and employee engagement second. Obviously, with agreement there is a platform for further diagnostic work and momentum for change.

Tip:
Holding an Engagement Summit

One approach to conducting diagnostic interviews is to convene group meetings. This approach has the particular benefit of simultaneously serving as a communications vehicle for executives to provide their support for the engagement campaign and involve the broader management team in the process. We refer to these meetings as engagement summits because of the connotation that the meeting is both out of the ordinary and that each of those attending is both expected to contribute and has an important view to be heard. These summits provide a forum for discussing what engagement means within the organization and its importance to organizational success. Importantly, as part of these meetings, participants should translate what engagement looks and feels like within their respective work groups. One way to orchestrate these meetings is to involve opinion leaders within the organization as engagement champions. Their range of influence is often far reaching and may be powerful in spreading the engagement message.

In summits held with leaders and managers, an important part of the summit should be the discussion of the behaviors and practices that they should specifically engage in as managers and leaders to help create a culture for engagement within their work groups. We talked about how to do this in the previous chapter on culture. Commitments on how participants will personally attempt to foster or sustain engagement should be made as well as part of these summits.

Step 3: Craft the Engagement Messaging

Choose the language around which you will communicate all aspects of the engagement campaign (and particularly the subsequent engagement survey and any distinct leadership survey efforts). Note that this can and should follow directly from the leadership team's purpose and the subsequent description of the local "look and feel" of engagement and how it contributes to organizational effectiveness. It is critical here to plan for this effort before rolling out the engagement campaign to the entire organization.

It is critical to test the messaging. One method is to put together several focus groups and test the actual messaging with them. This is probably best done using professionals trained in the focus group method. Often, that expertise may exist in the marketing function within the company. However, even casual conversations can pinpoint areas of concern. Some of the questions you want to ask are:

- When you [read/hear] this what do you think "engagement" means?
- What does is look like when the people you work with are engaged?
- Why do you believe company leaders have an interest in engagement?
- How do you believe others within the company will interpret this message?

This step is critical because in the absence of information regarding the purpose of the effort, employees are quite likely to misinterpret the intent; depending on levels of trust within the organization, they may attribute motives to the leadership team that will work against the success of the effort. Indeed, we sometimes find that leaders have deep and passionately held concerns about *not* using the term engagement because it doesn't fit their preferred way of communicating. That is fine. What is important is focusing on how employee energy is directed toward what creates competitive advantage and ensuring that the approach adopted has relevant and important local meaning.

It is very important here to understand that employees likely will see the "engagement survey" as being *another* survey and not something new. Depending on how survey data have been used in the past, it will be more or less difficult to convince employees this is something worthwhile. If employee surveys in the past have received little attention (no feedback, no action) there will be what we term "appropriate cynicism" as to what is likely to follow from the new survey. Without belaboring the point too much, if a culture of mistrust and unfairness exists when the survey is attempted, then it will be absolutely necessary for the leadership team to know precisely how it will handle the results of the survey and communicate that upfront to employees so they will willingly participate.

Case Scenario:
Engagement Messaging at
Harrah's Entertainment

One way to communicate effectively with managers is to develop a model around which the engagement message is constructed. The approach taken at Harrah's provides a good example. Nigel Martin, VP of HR at Harrah's, described to us how it is done.[4]

The key to making engagement happen at Harrah's is to align messaging around engagement by centering the message on employees' needs. They put it succinctly: "Get Me, Guide Me, Root for Me." These become guiding principles for how managers are to behave, their training, and performance appraisal. Figure 4.1 shows the way Harrah's presents these guiding principles to managers, and items in their employee survey tap the degree to which employees find these activities present for them in their work.

The elegance in this approach is that all facets of engagement, from measurement to action, are summarized succinctly with a direct call for action. Of course the reality of implementation is more difficult, but it portrays simultaneously all of the following to managers: People are important, and you'd best keep them at the top of your mind if you want them to be engaged. Figure 4.2 shows some of the ways in which Harrah's says improvements in employee engagement can happen and the things managers are charged with making happen to ensure employees are engaged.

Harrah's uses the employee engagement survey to drive home the message. The survey provides one method for continual monitoring of the level of employee engagement. Key to the campaign's success is the follow-through with the survey results. Following each administration of their survey a newsletter is sent to senior managers in all of their properties where properties are compared in rank order from top to bottom on an engagement index. As Nigel Martin noted, this provides a natural competitiveness, but it is not just about the numbers. Managers are then not only challenged to make necessary improvements but, as indicated earlier, they are provided with the model to use as a basis for thinking about change (Figure 4.1) and some of the techniques for making change happen (Figure 4.2). They strive for continuous improvement because they recognize that they must never claim to have succeeded at engagement; it is an ongoing commitment to try to do more.

Cont.

The guiding principles of "Get Me. Guide Me. Root For Me." will be at the core of everything we do.

Get Me

- Take the time to know me
  - Know my aspirations
  - Know how I work best
  - Know how I learn
  - Know what inspires me
- Respect and understand my strengths and opportunities
- Be aware of my challenges
- Understand how to motivate me

Guide Me

- Show me what success looks like
- Provide me with coaching, tools and resources for success
- Make the path forward clear and well lit
- Protect me along the way

Root For Me

- Be my biggest fan
- Celebrate my success
  - Bring me to the attention of others when I succeed
- Challenge me to be better than I ever thought I could be
- Create and environment where I can succeed
- Commit yourself to my development

Figure 4.1 "How do we bring employee engagement to life?"

Alignment will be critical as we push forward on our Employee Engagement initiatives.
The guiding principles of "Get me, Guide Me, Root For Me" will be integrated into everything we do.

Leadership

- Leadership clinics
  - Continued focus on talent review follow up actions
- Leadership suite
  - Talent radar
  - Mentorship program
  - Emerging leaders summit
  - Executive development modules
  - High-potential rotational program

Talent acquisition

- "Branding" the employment process
  - All-Star campaign (attract and source the best possible talent)
  - Recruiter certification training
  - "Best in Class" panel auditions
- Diversity networks

Training

- Entertainment-themed new hire orientation
  - Testing at several properties in August
  - Broad rollout in September/October
- Branded online training portal
  - Reinforces emerging employee brand
- Coaching module

Performance culture

- Updated EOS/SFS
  - Deliver on EYB and GGR principles
  - Continuous Improvement Plans
- Revised Performance Appraisal process
  - Tool that drives business performance, focusing on *what & how*
  - Features leadership competencies woven throughout other pillars

Rewards & recognition

- Wellness initiatives
- Bonus/"Pay for Performance" closely linked to performance appraisal process
- Rewards council

Figure 4.2 "Engagement next steps: Professional best"

The Engagement Survey

Surveys are an efficient way to capture employees' views on issues. With the promise of anonymity and confidentiality that typically comes with surveys, employees tend to provide more open and honest feedback than they would if asked the same questions by other means where their identity is known. Think of your employees as front line reporters, telling you about what is really happening when "the rubber meets the road." Surveys provide executives with unfiltered information and data – employees' views on how they feel, and how the organization works or fails to work – data to which executives otherwise might not have access. It's been said that feedback is a gift. Survey feedback is especially so because it is unfiltered.

Creating a survey to measure engagement and the work environment conditions that support it requires us to think differently and break from past survey traditions that measure employee satisfaction or even commitment. There are important practical implications of focusing on what drives engagement as opposed to what drives satisfaction. We will speak to how driver analyses are conducted later in Chapter 5. For now, though, it is sufficient to point out we have replicated this pattern of results over time, with different clients, and in aggregate across national samples of data. What drives satisfaction are factors like job security, benefits, and opportunity for a "better" job. What drives engagement is the chance to use one's skills, a clear link between one's work and company objectives, and the encouragement to innovate. While the specific items that appear as drivers are not identical from client to client – in part because of differences in the items included in those surveys, and likely due in part to different workforce compositions – the nature of the drivers of satisfaction and engagement are consistent. We consistently find that the drivers of satisfaction are issues that pertain to what the organization provides to the employee, whereas the drivers of engagement involve the factors that impact the employee's ability to maximize her contribution to the company.

This important distinction has several implications for what gets done in organizations. First, successful efforts to improve on those things that impact engagement are more likely to increase team and organizational productivity. Taking full advantage of employees' skills, communicating how the work they perform contributes to company objectives, and encouraging them to bring new ideas forward through fair practices and procedures are clearly actions that are in the best interests of the employer and employee alike. On the other hand, guaranteeing job security, improving employee benefits, and increasing promotion opportunities clearly pertain to *employees'* needs more than they directly influence organizational success. Further, improving these things simply may not be feasible for companies due to financial and other constraints. Lifetime employment is a disappearing or extinct concept in most industries, and the rate at which health care costs are rising makes satisfaction with benefits harder and harder for companies to maintain, let alone improve. Therefore, we would expect initiatives proposed to address the issues that drive engagement to be more welcomed by executives and more beneficial to companies than those targeting the drivers of satisfaction.

Thus, from an action planning perspective, the drivers of engagement can be more easily influenced at the immediate manager level. In many contexts, low-level to mid-level managers can greatly influence the degree to which their direct reports' skills are fully utilized and their ideas are solicited and implemented, for example. On the contrary, influencing the drivers of satisfaction more likely requires corporate-level change. While a manager can influence whether an employee is terminated due to poor performance, he likely cannot directly prevent layoffs or improve his employees' benefits package. Although he can ensure fairness in promotion decisions, in most situations he can't promote most or all of his direct reports.

Key driver analyses such as those we've discussed are a primary method used in employee survey research to determine the issues on which to focus improvement efforts. It is quite evident that a company's choice to include a satisfaction (whether labeled as satisfaction or engagement) or engagement measure in their employee survey has a significant impact on the decisions and actions that result from the survey. Furthermore, for the reasons mentioned above, we believe that engagement, conceptualized as a state of urgency, focus, and intensity, is more critical to individual and company performance than is satisfaction with its meaning and connotations of satiation and contentment.

It is worth emphasizing one further distinction between measures of satisfaction and engagement. We distinguished in Chapter 2 the difference between thinking about engagement in terms of the broad kinds of behaviors that represent an engaged workforce and those that are strategically focused. Practically, this translates to our recommendation that your employee engagement measure should not only assess the general feelings of engagement and general engagement behaviors but also strategically focused behaviors. As HR strategists Becker, Huselid, and Ulrich have noted in their description of human resources practices in general, it is when HR practices are strategically focused that they are likely to facilitate specific competitive advantage – the same is true for employee engagement measures.[5]

It is important to emphasize that thinking about engagement doesn't mean that employee satisfaction or employee well-being is ignored. On the contrary, engaged employees tend to be satisfied. People want to do meaningful work and contribute to organizational success. Also, the interventions that create the conditions for meaningful work and enhance the capacity of employees to engage can have a positive effect on satisfaction as well.

Good to Know:
Common Survey Response Formats

The typical engagement survey includes a series of statements to which people can agree or disagree, often measured on a 5 point scale (strongly disagree = 1; disagree = 2; neither agree nor disagree = 3; agree = 4; strongly agree = 5). Questions may also be asked directly as to how satisfied they are with a particular component or outcome of their work (e.g., "how satisfied are you with ... ?"), or ask them to rate an object of opinion on a scale from poor to good, and so on.

Writing Questions that Focus on the Feelings of Engagement

We have stressed repeatedly that the feelings of engagement lead to the behaviors that create competitive advantage. By asking questions that directly tap the feelings of engagement in the survey, we will later be able to drill down empirically to determine what key factors drive those feelings for the employees of a company, figuratively peeling back the onion to get to the core of what is important to address in subsequent action planning and interventions.

The specific components of "feeling engaged" relevant for the engagement survey include: (a) a sense of goal-directed energy; (b) the feeling of focus and absorption or being lost in one's work; (c) a sense of enthusiasm and excitement about the contribution one is making; (d) a feeling of intense focus on the job. These components translate into questions (statements to which survey respondents agree or disagree) such as:

- I feel confident that I can meet my goals.
- I am excited about how my work matters to our team and the company.
- Time goes by very quickly when I am at work.
- I find it very easy to stay focused on what is most important for me to accomplish at work.

Writing Questions that Focus on Behavioral Engagement

In what we think of as "good" engagement surveys, both feelings of engagement and behavioral engagement are represented – employees are asked to report both on what they feel and what they see in the form of behavior happening around them. We earlier focused on questions that tap the feelings of engagement. Our focus here is on the behavioral framework.

Though many types of survey items are framed with the individual's perspective at the core (e.g., items like, "I can focus on my work when the going gets tough", or "I am willing to give extended effort on the job"), we feel that items that measure engagement behaviors need to be framed with the work group as the referent for two significant reasons. First, competitive advantage comes not through the talent or actions of individual employees one at a time, but through the organization's workforce as a whole, through the aggregate of individuals' efforts. Simply put, we are concerned with an engaged workforce, not an engaged individual one at a time. In fact, it is worth examining the extent to which employees within the unit agree on the level of engagement they see within the team or unit. For example, we know that the degree of consensus on employee-based measures of service climate predicts customer satisfaction above and beyond the simple average level of service climate within the work unit –

when people agree more on what the climate is, you get better predictions of what customers say about their level of satisfaction.[6] Similarly, teams perform better when there is greater consensus as well as a higher level of average fairness perceptions within the group.[7]

Second, and admittedly more tactical, the prospect of any one individual's responses to items being biased is of some concern. That is, one's responses to items related to whether they personally act engaged could be distorted due to demand characteristics (that is, responding as you think others would expect) or even due to self-preservation. So, for example we would expect the averages on self-report measures of, for example, staying focused at work to be higher on average than when people are reporting on the behavior of others with regard to how proactive they are or how persistent they are. In addition, when we ask a number of people in a work group to report on what is happening there, the aggregate or average of what they have to say yields a reliable indicator of what is actually going on there. For these reasons, items that measure whether employees act engaged should be framed in terms of what people see within their work groups, with a lead-in like, "Within my work group ..." or "The people I work with ...".

Tip:
Matching Survey Questions to Outcomes

The idea of matching the content of survey questions to the outcomes (service, safety, innovation) of interest has a long and useful history in psychometrics – the science behind the design of attitude survey measures, measures of personality, and all other forms of measurement. Psychologists and authors of a seminal book on attitude theory and research, Fishbein and Ajzen[8] long ago, for example, showed that attitude surveys best predict behavior when the survey items assessed feelings about a particular object of behavior. For example, if we want to predict racist behavior, don't just ask questions about attitudes towards others but about attitudes towards others of specific racial heritage. Similarly there is a good research tradition that shows that personality tests predict behavior at work best when the personality test questions ask about how people see themselves at work – not how they see themselves in general.[9] Initially, research on organizational climate has also shown that generic climate measures do not reliably predict organizational performance but strategically focused climate measures do predict safety climate[10] and service climate.[11]

Crafting questions specific to the strategy Now that we know how we frame items that measure engagement behaviors, let's look at how the content of items might vary based on a firm's strategy. We can probably all think of firms that differentiate themselves on innovation (e.g., 3M, Sony), customer service (e.g., Nordstrom, Four Seasons) or operational efficiency/cost containment (e.g., Costco, Wal-Mart). What would engagement behaviors look like in each of these types of firms? Let's just contrast two of the strategies mentioned above – innovation versus operational efficiency/cost containment. We can conceive of some engagement behaviors that would serve both strategies. For example, in both strategies, you would want employees who feel safe to actively challenge the status quo and suggest new and improved ways of doing things. But the content of those suggestions would be different. That is, in the case of a company with a strategic focus on product innovation, we want employees to propose the creation of new products and services; in the case of a company with a strategic focus on operational efficiency/cost containment, we want suggestions for more streamlined methods of execution. So, even though the general behavior of making suggestions would be important in both, we propose that the content of the behavioral engagement items should be tailored to the specific context to increase its relevance and ensure that its focus or intent is not misunderstood. Having such specifically focused behavioral engagement items, in turn, helps to make the behavior more transparent to

---

Example:
Strategically Focused Behavioral Engagement Survey Items

Innovation engagement behaviors: The people I work with maintain their focus on coming up with new products and services even when they encounter potential distractions.

vs.

Cost containment/operational efficiency engagement behaviors: The people I work with maintain their focus on proposing new ways to reduce costs and to be more efficient even when they encounter potential distractions.

vs.

Generic engagement behaviors: The people I work with maintain their focus at work even when they encounter potential distractions.

all, which is important as a basis for later driving improvement efforts.

It is very important to note, however, that there are some engagement behaviors that are not equally relevant across organizations. For example, an important engagement behavior for the innovation strategy, but perhaps less so for the cost containment one, would be the active pursuit of self-development activities that educate and train people to be more innovative and creative. Similarly, we can identify engagement behaviors that might fit the firm focused on operational efficiency and cost containment, but not innovation (e.g., minimizing waste and defects).

Just as firms differentiate themselves on strategy, divisions or functions within a firm may similarly differentiate themselves. In organizations where this is particularly true, they may find it useful to have similar frames of reference (engagement behaviors) and similar behaviors (for example, maintaining focus despite potential obstacles) but to frame these behaviors with a different focus/context by division or function as shown in the example box. This suggests that a common survey (for the most part) might be used in different functions across a company but with content appropriate for the strategic imperatives of those functions as the strategic behavioral focus of the items. The need for this kind of adaptation in survey content should be balanced with the value that also comes from having a company-wide completely universal metric.

Writing questions that focus on the connection between work and strategy The answers to strategically focused engagement questions will tell you whether or not people see engagement being played out strategically in the organization. Other more general questions about the feelings of engagement and engagement behaviors will give further insight into engagement levels within the company or work unit. As we suggested earlier, it is also important to know if employees understand the link between what they do and the strategy of the firm. This is a question of employee–organization alignment. Questions of the type we have found useful include items such as:

- There is a clear link between what I do and organizational objectives.
- I have a good idea of what my company is trying to accomplish.

Writing Generic Behavioral Engagement Survey Questions

Although the strategic focus of the firm determines the specific ways in which engagement behavior takes form, there are more general manifestations of engagement behavior that serve as the background against which specific behaviors emerge. As pointed out in Chapter 2, these include factors such as proactivity, persistence, role expansion, and adaptability. Thus, representative questions of this more general type include:

- The people in my work group fix little problems before they become major issues.
- The people here look for ways to improve the way we work.
- The norm here is to stay with a problem until you get it solved.
- The people here take on new responsibilities as the need arises.

You can see that these are more generic characterizations of an engaged workforce and are important to be sure – but that it would be also important to know how these get played out in the form of specific strategically relevant behaviors given specific jobs.

Writing Questions that Focus on Creating the Employee Capacity to Engage

The question of whether individuals have the capacity to engage seems fundamental. If people don't possess the energy to engage in their work or don't have the basic resources and tools needed to engage, there can obviously be no engagement. Consistent with contemporary uses of the term, such "capital" can be social, informational or structural, and psychological. Some of this people bring with them from outside work. Some of this can be developed, enhanced, or depleted at work. From a diagnostic perspective, we are interested in those factors that can be influenced through intervention. These fall into three categories:

1 individual sources of energy and vigor, or psychological capital;
2 necessary financial, informational, and physical resources to do the work; and
3 social support within the team and organization.

Individual sources of energy and vigor While these can include both dispositional factors (psychological traits) and also less permanent "mind sets," our interest is restricted to the latter, simply because our focus is on what can be changed through intervention. The specific factors that are embraced within this notion of "mind set" arguably include many, but from our perspective these factors have at their core the notion of what psychologists call "agency," or the capacity to achieve success, i.e., reach a goal through one's own effort and means. In the context of the work environment and employee engagement, this means the belief that one can overcome obstacles, that persistence will make a difference, and that one is sufficiently competent to do the task at hand. In short, agency is about the very notion of what we mean by engagement – moving forward and getting things done as well as the emotional state of positive affect.[12]

Within a diagnostic context, we think the relevant questions of interest address whether the organization and its leaders contribute to that mind set. Particularly relevant are questions regarding communications and leadership practices that encourage the sense of optimism and hope that people have for the future. To understand how this plays out, consider a point in time where two companies are considering a merger. Within one company, employees share the view that the other company will be the "winner." Hallway talk is of who will lose their jobs, whose work will be displaced, and what life will be like after the merger. Here, there is a fundamental lack of optimism or any belief that the future company can be a compelling place to work.

In our other company, there is a sense of excitement over the pending deal. Here, the hallway talk is about the opportunities for personal growth and company success. You can envision the sense of energy and purpose with which people approach their work. These employees are in a very different "state of mind." It is such a state of mind, reflected in the notions of hope, optimism, resiliency, and other related psychological states that are fundamental to engagement. This is not a question of whether personal energy can be released or targeted; it is a question of whether that energy can be found.

Some of the kinds of questions relevant to the factors that create the sense of resiliency, optimism, and hope within such a merger context would include:

- I feel confident in the future of our business.
- I have the skills I need to meet the future demands of my job.
- We have done the planning in our work group to make the transition with new management a success.

Some examples of questions serving as more general examples include:

- I have been adequately trained to do my job.
- My supervisor helps me to develop confidence in my own ability to do my job well.
- My supervisor sets challenging but achievable goals.
- My supervisor supports my need to balance my work and personal life.

Resources The second kind of necessary resources are those that people simply need to do their jobs: Tools, information, equipment, and the like. Relevant survey questions might include:

- I have enough information to do my job well.
- My work group has the resources (finances, equipment, etc.) necessary to do high quality work.

It is not uncommon for engagement surveys to drill down using more specific questions about specific kinds of resources and communication issues. We see these kinds of issues as providing a foundation for engagement feelings and behavior as it is difficult to be fully engaged when you do not have the wherewithal to do the work.

Social support Finally, a third resource is the availability of social support necessary to work effectively in the business. Often, our clients think of these as the issues centering on the facilitating component of teamwork but our engagement framework extends somewhat further. Specifically, the positive affect and emotional state that coincides with the energy and vigor visible to others arises directly in a social/work context.[13] Diagnostic questions in the engagement survey would include items like:

- The people I work with cooperate to get the job done.
- I can count on the people I work with to help me if needed.

Writing Questions that Focus on Whether People Have a Reason to Engage

In Chapter 2 we presented in significant detail the importance of meaningful work for the feelings of engagement. We defined this earlier as work that has challenge and variety, allows for autonomy, and provides people with feedback. In addition, work that is aligned with one's values and seen as contributing to the company's success contributes to feelings that one's work is meaningful. Survey items ought to reflect these notions. Some examples of relevant survey questions include:

- My job makes good use of my skills and abilities.
- I feel encouraged to come up with new and better ways of doing things.
- The people who work here share common values.
- The work we do is important to me.

Much of what comprises the current interest in employee attitudes toward social responsibility of organizations is relevant in this context. We introduce this because much of what can be done to influence employee perceptions of the "corporate brand" can be thought of as not just issues of what drives the employee value proposition but also what provides a purpose for engagement. For example, the Sun Microsystems corporate website includes a specific reference to corporate social responsibility under the section of its website titled "employee engagement." One Sun employee, quoted on that webpage answered the question "When I say socially and environmentally responsible, I mean:" with "not just saying the words as marketing hype but actually incorporate it into our company's DNA in how to conceive/architect/design/deliver products and services."[14]

So, relevant questions for the engagement survey might include:

- Decisions at my company are made in a socially and environmentally responsible fashion.

- My company actively contributes to the communities in which we do business.

It is worth noting that the kind of meaningful relationship people seek to find with and through their employer is a source for the sense of pride that many confuse with engagement. That is, pride is not such a manifestation of engagement itself as it is an outcome of working in a company that serves a meaningful purpose and is linked to a larger sense of purpose and meaning in life.

Writing Questions that Focus on Whether People Feel "Free" to Engage

We've emphasized repeatedly that trust and fairness are critical conditions for engagement to emerge. From a diagnostic perspective, this is a question of whether people can feel safe to engage; that their efforts will be worthwhile (recognized and supported) and in particular not put them in a disadvantageous position or at risk.

While trust often appears in employee opinion surveys, it isn't generally given the emphasis that we think it deserves. A single item or two, often geared only at trust in upper management, is not sufficient to capture the complexity and multi-layered meanings and foci of trust as we see it. Even if there are multiple items on trust, the perspective is nearly always one-sided – do employees trust others (their managers, leaders, co-workers)? What isn't typically included is whether employees *feel trusted*. Yet, this is critical for them to feel safe, and without feeling safe to engage, employees are unlikely to suggest new and innovative ways of doing things, go "off process" to meet a unique customer need, and so on.

Some example questions of "feeling trusted" and "psychologically safe" include:

- I feel safe to speak my mind about how things can be improved.
- I can take action to satisfy a customer without worrying about being second-guessed by my manager.
- I can count on my supervisor to back me up on the actions I take to address a customer's dissatisfaction.

Similarly, while fairness may be assessed, its treatment too tends to be limited both in terms of the number of items included and in the focus of these items. We've seen surveys where there are a number of items that assess fairness. The problem is that they focus on a single type of fairness ("I feel fairly treated here"). Ideally, an engagement survey would include items specific to the types of fairness that we discussed in the previous chapter – outcomes (e.g., satisfaction with recognition received in the form of rewards or public praise), procedural (e.g., clear links made between decisions and the procedures that led to them), and interpersonal (e.g., treated with respect and dignity).

Good to Know:
The Measurement of Perceived Fairness[15]

Items that might assess overall fairness:

- Taking everything into account I feel fairly treated by this company
- Overall I feel this company is just and fair in the way it treats and rewards employees.

Items that might assess fairness of outcomes:

- In general the rewards I receive in this organization are fair.
- I feel the rewards I get are equitable given the work I do.

Items that might assess procedural fairness:

- Decisions here about people are made using fair procedures.
- The guidelines that exist for making decisions here are fair.

Items that might assess interactional fairness:

- My boss treats me fairly in the way s/he interacts with me
- My co-workers treat me fairly.

As we also discussed in detail in Chapter 3, the importance of fairness is that it provides a foundation for trust that, in turn, provides the foundations for feeling safe and ultimately behaving in engaged ways. The role of the immediate supervisor in this is shown clearly in the items in the Good to Know box, especially *vis-à-vis* interpersonal fairness.

Summary

An engagement survey, like all good things in organizations, requires attention and the devil is once again in the details. There are two important sets of details we addressed: (a) the process of the entire survey campaign; and (b) the content of the survey items. With regard to the campaign process, we emphasized the point that the

---

Good to Know:
Sample Survey Items to Measure Engagement

Items that measure engagement feelings:

- I feel confident that I can meet my goals.
- I am excited about how my work matters to our team and the company.
- Time goes by very quickly when I am at work.
- I find it very easy to stay focused on what is most important to accomplish at work.

Items that measure engagement behaviors (generic):

- The people in my work group fix little problems before they become major issues.
- The people here look for ways to improve the way we work.
- The norm here is to stay with a problem until you get it solved.
- The people here take on new responsibilities as the need arises.

Items that measure strategic engagement behaviors:

- The people I work with maintain their focus on coming up with new products and services even when they encounter potential distractions. (Innovation engagement behavior)
- The people I work with maintain their focus on proposing new ways to reduce costs and to be more efficient even when they encounter potential distractions. (Cost containment/ operational efficiency engagement behaviors)

Items that focus on the connection between work and strategy:

- There is a clear link between what I do and organizational objectives.
- I have a good idea of what my company is trying to accomplish.

Items that focus on creating the employee capacity to engage:

- I have been adequately trained to do my job.
- My supervisor helps me to develop confidence in my own ability to do my job well.
- My supervisor sets challenging but achievable goals.

senior leadership of the organization must come to some agreement on why employee engagement is important to the company and how they will know employee engagement when they see it. In the absence of such agreement the employee engagement survey process will fail to achieve objectives for at least some of the leadership team.

When we hear the words employee engagement survey, we think of the survey content and we provided a lot of detail about the kinds of content we feel it is important to have in such a survey. See the "Sample Survey Items to Measure Engagement" box for a recap of suggested item content.

Thus to our way of thinking, here are the points to ensure: (a) the content should be strategically focused; (b) the content should focus on behavior since that is what we want to change; (c) the content should focus on the immediate causes (trust and fairness) of feeling safe that serve as the foundation of behavioral engagement; (d) the content should include the factors that establish the source of energy people bring to work; and (e) the content should include the factors that make people want to invest that energy into their work.

Chapter 5

Phase 2 of Creating and Executing an Engagement Campaign: Action Planning and Intervention

In the previous chapter we focused on the initial stages of an engagement campaign including background preparation of the organization and the engagement survey itself. Our emphasis was on developing an engagement survey that would tap both engagement feelings and behaviors as well as the conditions (fairness, trust, job design) that determine whether engagement can and will emerge.

We focus now on how the results of surveys can be used to drive the kinds of changes that yield a more engaged and more competitive workforce. Specifically, we discuss in some detail a series of interrelated issues:

- how to interpret survey results in ways that will prove useful;
- providing feedback to all of the relevant stakeholders in organizations and not just to executives and management;
- preparing the organization to take action based on the results and feedback; and
- specific actions organizations can take to increase employee engagement.

We go into considerable detail on these issues because many companies think of an engagement survey as the questions you ask, followed by some vague thoughts about how to use the results obtained. Such vagueness can greatly undermine an engagement survey *process*; the entire *process* must be handled effectively for anything good to come from the survey. We present lots of detailed steps below to help make this process effective – and to improve the employee engagement that contributes to competitive advantage for organizations.

Survey Results Interpretation

In our view, the engagement scores themselves are important, but they don't focus attention on the critical things that management should attend to in their efforts to drive engagement. A well-designed engagement survey provides a great deal of data to help focus attention where it will be most useful. This guidance is of course critical given the many competing demands on managers' time.

Benchmarks

You look at the survey results and then you interpret them: What's high and what's low and you move on from there, right? Not quite. The question is better framed as: compared to what benchmark or benchmarks are the results high or low?

Just about all companies use results from prior administrations of their employee surveys as a benchmark against which they begin to interpret current results. Over time then, companies accumulate a wealth of internal benchmark data they can use to ask questions like: Have survey results improved where we took action? For example, if supervisors were given training to help them treat their employees in more fair and equitable ways, do the survey results reveal any improvement with regard to such questions on the survey?

Our experience in organizations suggests that comparisons to previous administrations of a survey are important, but they are only one way to interpret results and have their limitations. Thus, over the many opportunities we have had to meet with executives and discuss survey results, one common question emerges: "Where do we stand compared to others?" Some have called this a "report card mentality" but it does reflect the reality that executives want to know how they stack up relative to other firms. Executives immediately grasp that what is high and low depends on the frame of reference used to answer the question. So, it is very useful to have some perspective when looking at results. While there can be real value in benchmarks, the value is only as good as the benchmark itself. An anecdote may help to illustrate this.

Some years ago, we were presenting a company's overall results to the CEO of a major company and a few members of his team. We'll call this company ABC for present purposes. In previous years, based on a benchmark that was an aggregation of its previous consulting firm's clients' data, a rather negative picture of their survey results was presented. Results were interpreted relative to this benchmark and considerable time and organizational resources went to addressing "opportunity areas" – items with low scores relative to this benchmark.

Imagine the CEO's surprise to learn that ABC's results actually fared well relative to your authors' benchmark – a benchmark based on surveying employees who worked for companies listed on Fortune's *Best Companies to Work For* and *Most Admired* lists. Which benchmark was right? Clearly, he thought ours was more compelling. We like to think that this is because it represents best-in-class firms and passes other tests of quality (e.g., stability over time). One could argue that he preferred our benchmark because it portrayed ABC's results more favorably. Regardless, the point is that not all benchmark comparisons will give comparable information. It's important to choose benchmark comparisons carefully, based on the quality of the benchmark and its relevance to the firm; otherwise, you may squander limited corporate resources addressing issues that aren't critical to address.[1]

Also important is "selling" this benchmark internally within organizations. A benchmark can be a powerful tool in helping others understand where the company is being successful and where change is needed. Similarly, the benchmark helps to frame just how much change might be possible. However, for a benchmark to serve these roles, the organization's executive team and managers need to view it as a compelling benchmark that is relevant to them.

While we believe that benchmarks play a valuable role in interpreting survey data, using them to set targets for improvement ought to be done with some care. As corporate strategists Kaplan and Norton pointed out in describing Balanced Scorecard companies: "target-setting with the Balanced Scorecard starts with aspirations for radical performance breakthroughs in financial and customer outcome measures. *Balanced Scorecard Companies expect to become the benchmark for others.* The targets for near-term performance are determined not by individual process benchmarks, but by what the organization must achieve in the short run to remain on a trajectory to longer-term performance breakthroughs."[2]

In short, one does not go from a company aspiring to achieve benchmarking status to that status overnight. Rather, achieving benchmark status is a process with intermediate goals and it is the choice of those intermediate goals that is the challenge early in the campaign. And, not to belabor the point too much, it is the ways engagement survey data are used that help achieve those intermediate steps and eventual benchmark status over time.

Survey Results Feedback

Based both on anecdotal experience and hard data, we know that organizations who invest time and effort in providing survey feedback are most likely to gain the benefits from the survey effort. The companies who find engagement surveys to be a worthwhile investment recognize that one of the key phases in an engagement survey campaign is to disseminate results. Here is the rule: Executives, managers and employees alike have expectations that results will be reported back to them in a timely manner. In fact, expectations are likely heightened in cases where the survey provides metrics that have a life outside the survey itself, such as part of a workforce or balanced scorecard or as input into performance evaluations or a talent review process.

Typically, results are reported first to senior management, and then rolled out throughout the organization. Regardless of the roll-out strategy, well-designed presentations and report formats facilitate interpretation and the action planning process that follows. Organizing results around an engagement model can help in this regard, particularly to the extent that this model has been well-communicated and accepted within the organization.

A typical engagement survey administration results in a great deal of data. The interested reader who wants to learn more about the variety of ways in which data can be reported should consult any one of a number of good sources on the topic.[3] Our own experience has taught us that different approaches to reporting may be required for different stakeholder audiences.

Feedback at the Executive Level

At the executive level, the data must be credible, defensible and strategic, presenting a dashboard-like summary of results with emphasis given to key metrics. Executive level reports often differ from those used at other levels of the organization because they are briefer and more succinct. Scorecard views comparing divisions, geographies, or key functions on major survey categories or key metrics are commonly included in executive level reports. In addition, reports for executives more consistently highlight gaps from external benchmark comparisons, where available, and may even include multiple external benchmarks (e.g., industry-specific and a "best companies" type norm). Results are often positioned within a model of engagement like the value chain framework presented in Chapter 1. Finally, a high level view of results for key employee segments is often a component of these reports (e.g., how the organization's "A" talent or high performers responded, gender differences, and for geographically dispersed companies, how different locations responded world-wide).

With all of the detail available in survey data, it is easy to forget that the purpose of the survey is diagnostic and is only one step in the engagement campaign. In the end, what is important is to identify what can be done to enhance workforce engagement and so we must discover what the key drivers of engagement may be. This is a question of *relative priority* or *impact*. Of course, "impact" begs the question of "impact on what?" The choice matters. For example, we know from frequent experience that most executives equate employee retention with engagement. Without the kinds of framing conversations we described in the previous chapter, they will not recognize that the drivers of turnover intentions can in fact be different from the drivers of strategic engagement. Impact is typically determined by conducting a "key driver analysis." These analyses use one form or another of statistical regression analysis and depend on the strength of statistical relationship between the other questions in the survey with an engagement index based on the aggregate scores of the relevant engagement items. So, if there are five questions in the engagement index, the average of these items is calculated for each survey respondent and then correlated with each of the potential drivers which are represented in the other survey questions [e.g., questions pertaining to one's relationship with their supervisor(s), fairness of treatment, availability of necessary resources (tools and equipment)]. The outcome of this analysis is then the relative strength of relationship between these potential drivers and engagement, which are then rank-ordered from high to low; those on the high end are the likely first targets of intervention – they have the highest "impact." We have to say without elaboration that there are serious statistical issues to be considered in conducting such analyses and that all methods are not equal in providing useful results.[4]

In the final analysis, what managers and executives need to know is where to invest their time and energy. One highly familiar form for helping to answer this question is to classify the drivers of engagement in relative terms (e.g., high vs. low) and cross-tabulate against actual group/company results (i.e., high or low in absolute terms, or perhaps relative to a benchmark). An example of this familiar kind of analysis is shown in Figure 5.1. We should emphasize that while the world seems fixated on simplifying everything to the 2 x 2 quadrant analysis, such presentations do fill the need of answering the question "What should I look at first?" and are becoming more common in presenting survey results.

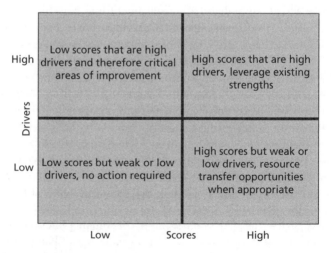

Figure 5.1 Quadrant analysis

Feedback at the Managerial Level

For managers, reports should provide sufficient detail to ensure that they have concrete data to use as a basis for producing practical action plans at their local level. The best reports use a combination of text and visual displays to appeal to different individual preferences for data presentation and help to cut through the detail. Our experience suggests some features or approaches that help to ease interpretation:

- *Highlight noteworthy results*, such as large changes over time or large differences from internal/external benchmarks, with easy-to-understand symbols (e.g., a "red flag" connotes exactly that).
- *Provide managers with thought starters to ask themselves* to understand better why employees responded as they did, particularly for areas identified as opportunities. For example, in response to low results on an item pertaining to the link between one's work and company objectives, the following thought starters might be provided: "How do you communicate the company's objectives to employees? How do you confirm their understanding? What have you done to show employees how their work contributes to the company's success?"
- *Embed specific suggestions for action* to address opportunity areas within the report to help jump-start action planning. A concern with this approach is that these action steps may be blindly accepted without careful consideration of what steps might be best suited to address a concern. Therefore, appropriate caveats ought to be given over their use. In addition, suggestions that come from consultants and survey researchers may not appreciate the nuances involved in implementing the suggestion and managers can view the suggestions as infeasible, not appropriate, or worse as coming from uninformed people. For these reasons, it is advisable to base recommendations on empirical evidence and to provide the accompanying thought starters so that managers can evaluate the appropriateness of a suggestion for a specific context. Having clients review the best practices in a consultant's offering is also advised to ensure that they are appropriate and relevant to their context.

The important point for feedback of results to this level of management is that it is at this level where action *vis-à-vis* engagement can have the greatest impact. Thus, issues of fairness, trust, leadership, job design and support (both social and technical) are controllable here so it is critical that managers have some help in getting the conversation started that will produce recommendations for actual change.

Communicating Survey Results Company-Wide

After having participated in a survey, employees will expect that results will be shared with them and acted upon. In fact, as PepsiCo corporate psychologists Allan Church and David Oliver put it, by doing a survey, we implicitly enter into a social contract with employees that management cares about their feedback *and is willing to act on it.*[5] The failure to share results *and* take action can result in a loss of trust in management and cynicism over future survey efforts. Sharing results company-wide and not just with senior management or even local management is a visible sign that senior management is attending to results and is one important component in helping to provide a firm foundation from which to drive change. In essence, communication of survey results is a "trust sustainable."

Company-wide results are typically communicated through formal means to ensure that the same message is delivered to all employees. Formally communicating results gives senior management the opportunity to:

- Highlight significant areas of strengths as well as challenges and to comment on any company-wide initiatives either underway or being considered to address these issues.
- Reflect on and celebrate progress made in response to challenges identified in the previous survey administration, if relevant.
- Present data on how employees are thinking about strategic initiatives about which they may have heard or might have been asked.
- Give recognition to those organizational groups whose actions in response to the last survey resulted in the most meaningful changes. In cases where progress overall has not met expectations, a sober review of this is necessary with a renewed commitment to address the issues that appear to be the most salient drivers.

Though informational, a key aspect of these formal communications is to paint a picture for the need for change where necessary and to enlist all in the efforts that will be required. Thus, these communications should reinforce the importance of action planning at all levels, and emphasize each employee's role in the change process. But remember to note the strengths, too, since strengths can be built on.

Good to Know:
Focusing on the Positives

It is too easy and too usual for consultants and executives to focus on the low scores, the bad scores, in surveys. That is, if a survey is used as a basis for making change, don't we need to focus on what needs changing? Well, yes, but not only there. Guess what: Focusing on the negatives makes the survey a negative psychologi- cal experience for those taking it and for those charged with improving it. Most companies do many things right or they would not be in business. When providing feedback, emphasize the positive, too, and ask how you can use what you are doing well to make improvements where they are needed.[6]

Company-wide results may be communicated through a variety of means, the more the merrier since people differ in the media to which they pay close attention. Some communication channels include the following:

- Overview of results in the company newsletter. This might take the form of a letter from the CEO.
- A video, web, or podcast presentation of the CEO sharing key results.
- Town hall meetings in which the CEO or other members of senior management share the results with groups of employees and respond to questions.
- Special publications (e.g., brochures) distributed to all employees. Note that such publications must be cautiously produced since they can become public and therefore should contain only what the company wishes to have made public.

• Posters highlighting strengths and opportunities for display in team work areas.

Summary

The design of the engagement survey itself and its administration is not the end of a process but the beginning. Providing the gift of feedback is the second phase of the process with somewhat different methods used for the various stakeholders to the survey: executives, senior management, local management, and company-wide to employees. We have continually reinforced the importance of creating a culture of trust and fairness as fundamental to the sense of safety, which in turn enables employees to fully invest themselves in their work. Providing *and acting on* survey feedback is one way in which the organization demonstrates that it trusts employees to understand and act on survey results. In the absence of such feedback to employees, management fuels appropriate cynicism and once such cynicism emerges, it will be very difficult to overcome.

Preparing the Organization for Taking Action[7]

One of the most difficult parts of a survey process is ensuring that the results lead to positive change. Simply put, it is often worse to

---

Example:
The Importance of Taking Action

Allan Church and David Oliver[8] of PepsiCo demonstrated the value of taking action on survey results in a large-scale global survey. They found that overall employee satisfaction scores were highest for locations where employees reported that results were shared and acted upon (78%); in contrast, overall satisfaction scores were lowest in locations where employees said that results were not acted upon (51%), with equivalent levels shown regardless of whether results were shared and not acted upon or not shared and not acted upon. Further, locations where results were shared and acted upon showed the most improvement over time. Finally, they linked taking action on survey results to bottom-line business metrics for one division. Locations where the majority of employees reported that action was taken on survey results had fewer safety incidents and lost days due to accidents as well as lower turnover. While the focus here was on improving employee satisfaction, it shows the importance of using survey results to drive change.

ask employees for their input and then ignore it, than it is to never ask them at all (see the Example box on the importance of taking action).

The box shows some of the positive consequences from providing feedback and taking action so it raises the questions of what it means to take action, by whom, and how. In this part of the chapter we show you how to get ready to take action. Getting the commitment for action prior to conducting the survey is a critical component of the engagement campaign.

Commitment for Action

Who should be responsible for action planning? While the survey may originate as a HR/other initiative, ultimate responsibility for using the results and driving change must reside with line management, with the appropriate support and guidance from their HR partners. At the end of the day, only managers can provide the time and resources needed to implement action plans and it is managers who are in touch with the people who do the work – the people we need to have engaged.

Without a commitment for action planning among managers and those designated to support the process (e.g., HR generalists, OD specialists), we have seen the process quickly derail. Fortunately, there are many ways to build and sustain commitment to using survey results to drive change including:

- *Clearly demonstrate to managers and employees the value of employee engagement* and why the survey is being used as a means of driving change and measuring progress. Make certain that the messaging focuses on building a workplace that fosters engagement *and* well-being. Messaging needs to be continually reinforced and in terms that employees can understand and identify with.
- *Integrate the survey process with other business planning activities* to give it broader focus and emphasis. It should not be viewed as a stand-alone event but rather as an integral component of business planning. Including an engagement metric in workforce scorecards helps to highlight this connection. Use these measures not only to track engagement but as input into other decisions (e.g., budgeting decisions, promotions).

- *Ensure that the survey content – and any resulting indices or metrics – has high perceived relevance* within the organization. The survey should include items that are aligned with the company's values and strategic imperatives. Involving key stakeholders in the survey creation process can help to increase buy-in. The more the survey reads like it is relevant to employees and the company, the higher the response rate and the more valid the responses.[9]
- Further, *ensure that survey results are actionable on items for which managers are held responsible.* Obviously survey items tap into various levels of responsibility and can be outside the scope of the immediate work group. For example, some aspects of total rewards are outside unit-level management's purview so the results for which they can be held responsible should focus on issues over which they have control.
- *Clearly define accountability for sharing and using results.* Typically, the expectation is that managers will conduct survey feedback meetings to share the survey results. At a minimum here managers should share evidence about strengths that can be leveraged and opportunities to address. Then, two to three tangible and doable goals should be set and action plans are created to address these goals, all with input from employees.
- *Provide managers with the appropriate tools and support* to make their action planning efforts successful as described in the next section.

Resources and Tools That Facilitate Action Planning and Change

All too often, the action planning phase of survey initiatives is short-changed in the planning process, with a disproportionate amount of time and energy during planning going to survey design and administration and perhaps basic reporting of results. At its worst, action planning is treated somewhat as an afterthought. Yet, it takes time to put into place the appropriate resources and tools needed to support action planning; even if these are acquired through a vendor, time is needed to gain commitment for and effectively implement the action planning process. Psychologist and Wharton professor Katherine Klein has called this creating a climate for implementation – and this climate is mostly created by the resources that management actually provides to facilitate taking action and supporting change.[10]

What resources, tools and support should be provided to managers? This will depend upon the target audience and their experience in using survey results and creating action plans.

Good to Know:
The Target Audience

No one would dispute that training should be targeted to the level of the audience. Determining the appropriate level though can be difficult. At times, we've seen inappropriate assumptions made over the level and type of training needed with regard to interpreting and using survey data to drive improvement efforts. In retail-type environments, for example, we've seen training oversimplified for managers who routinely use data and implement action plans to manage their departments/branches. In contrast, we've seen training either significantly shortened or bypassed altogether for managers in corporate positions who are assumed to be more skilled in this process, but actually may need more guidance. Decisions about the type of training/support needed should not be based on pay grade or preconceived notions, but rather on managers' experience in using data to make decisions and drive change and, where possible, prior evidence on their effectiveness shown in earlier similar efforts.

However, beyond clear and easy to use report formats, some options include the following:

- Self-study guides, facilitated training programs, or e-learning programs to teach managers how to interpret survey results and facilitate survey feedback and action planning meetings with employees. Topics may cover guidelines for interpreting survey results and how to: integrate results and determine the most pressing priorities; set SMART (i.e., specific, measurable, actionable, realistic, and time-based) goals; develop effective action plans; and deal with difficult situations within the context of a feedback meeting.
- Resource banks with best practices and other resources (e.g., books, internal training programs, web-based resources) to help managers

identify possible action steps to take in addressing their issues. The idea here is to have best practices that are aligned with the survey content so managers are provided with some clues about how to proceed on issues that are shown to be opportunities. Best practice libraries may be purchased/licensed through vendors, developed internally, or a combination of the two (e.g., an external bank where managers can add their own organization-specific best practices). Some organizations prefer best practices gathered internally because of higher perceived relevance; externally developed best practices may be more comprehensive though and the best of these libraries base their best practices on the research literature for proven strategies. Regardless of whether they are developed internally or licensed, the quality of these resource banks can vary significantly and should be evaluated prior to implementation. It is important to review best practices to make sure that they are in fact actions that your organization wants to endorse as noted earlier in this chapter.

Example:
Safety Best Practices from Dov Zohar, Safety Climate Expert[11]

Suppose safety practices emerge as an opportunity for improvement in a company. Here are some best practices for managers to improve safety awareness and behavior:

- Develop and use a daily safety checklist and do a "walk-through" on a regular basis to look for unsafe behavior, practices, and conditions. Consult with employees (and unions) in developing the checklist and making these rounds as to issues of a safety and/or security nature they have observed or for which they have suggestions for improvement.
- Model and encourage all employees to engage in safe work practices and correct unsafe activities or conditions. Use observation of specific safe or unsafe behaviors as a chance to do training; catch people behaving safely and recognize and reinforce.
- Create an environment in which reporting safety/security issues that require attention is openly reinforced, honored, praised and recognized. This environment requires that employees trust supervisors to appreciate such feedback, that the feedback will be used and acted on, that it will NOT lead to embarrassment of the reporter, and that such reports are an important part of everyone's job.

- Access to sample action steps like those in the Dov Zohar Example box provide managers exemplars of well-developed plans, particularly proven plans to address common challenges. Managers may benefit from seeing the plans of others who have had success in addressing challenges similar to their own. These may be plans created in response to the current survey or examples of particularly effective plans from the previous survey administration.
- Online action planning tools to facilitate plan tracking and goal alignment throughout the organization. While action planning can be implemented without the benefit of an online system, these tools have the advantage of allowing plans to be more easily tracked and even shared. Without such a system, the administrative burden of gathering plans can be significant, which explains why few organizations have a centralized repository for them absent an online system. Besides, action plans should be "living documents" updated as progress is made or conditions change. A hard copy version is a single snapshot in time. Another advantage of online action planning tools is that they typically allow for goals to be cascaded throughout the organization thereby helping to ensure alignment. Further, some systems allow for suggestions to be submitted up one's management chain or to specific units or entities (e.g., IT, HR), somewhat like a suggestion box. The anonymous submission of suggestions might be particularly useful in organizations where open communications are a challenge and other mechanisms are lacking to gather similar information. Of course, if managers are allowed to escalate suggested goals, they should be coached to only escalate those that are outside of their direct control.

Variants on the Action Planning Model

Thus far, our focus has been on a very traditional action planning model – managers conduct survey feedback meetings with employees and together they create action plans. Variants of this approach have been used successfully. One variant is to create engagement teams that pull together the talents of the company's high potential employees to address organization-wide challenges identified as part of an engagement survey. The value of this approach comes from pulling together diverse talents drawn from various parts of the organization so that a broad, collective perspective on organizational issues is considered. This approach could serve as an action learning component in leadership programs, giving high potential employees an opportunity to gain additional practice in using data to drive decisions to solve management challenges.

How Much Measurable Change is Possible?

To this point, we've discussed how you can use survey results to diagnose key opportunity areas that can be addressed to enhance employee engagement. This begs the question of how much change is really possible. Senior leaders often expect and even demand rapid results; they likely have reached their levels in organizations by setting bold goals and delivering on them. So, it can be a challenge to help them set appropriate goals for how quickly and how much engagement will improve over time. As we've argued elsewhere in this book, driving engagement takes sustained effort and focus. Given all that needs to be done, it might not come as a surprise that dramatic improvements in engagement scores between survey administrations are not typical. Some of the specific reasons measurable change tends to be smaller than might be hoped for or even anticipated include:

- The relative difference between companies on an engagement norm is not huge; the difference between a company falling at the 75th percentile and one falling at the 25th percentile may be only on the order of 10 percentage points favorable on the engagement survey – but each one of those 10 points is associated with significant differences in financial outcomes as we showed in Chapter 1. So, if the engagement index for a company is at 65% favorable, moving to 70% favorable would be indeed a very significant measurable change.
- Items that are more locally actionable may show impressive change especially in units that have new managers because the prior manager was deficient. The rule is that the change can be the greatest where the scores are the poorest.
- Some changes simply don't impact everyone so the question is whether change happened where it needed to happen. Other changes impact people only infrequently but change is required there because of the criticality of the issue, e.g., an issue of safety.

The question then becomes, did the change occur even though the demand for the issue is infrequent. Further, some actions simply take time before their effects are evident. So, action plans shouldn't be abandoned in the absence of either immediate or dramatic measurable change.

· People don't believe change has occurred, regardless of the evidence (see the box on why change is so difficult).

Despite the "realism" we encourage among our clients, gains in the aggregate can be substantial and significant over successive years. And, it is with this longer-term horizon that targets should first be set and then translated into achievable goals for the shorter term.

Good to Know:
Why Change is So Difficult

Changing the actual results in employee surveys is very difficult because of the time lags involved in making change. Suppose you administer a survey in January and report back results in March. It may take time to roll results out throughout the organization to the appropriate management levels for action planning. Then, it might take additional time to set the action planning process in full motion – time to train managers and/or to set company-wide goals with which they can align. Before you know it, more time has passed and it might be July or August before groups begin to execute their action plans. The survey is administered again in January – before much of what is being done is seen to have an impact by employees.

Why does it take so long to have an impact? Because as people we are used to the steady state of the worlds in which we live and changes can be made yet be completely unnoticed by us. And if we notice them at all, we think of them as an aberration unless we repeatedly encounter them. Change requires repetition and then more repetition or else it will not be noticed or paid attention to.

All other things being equal, a gain of 5 percent favorable points is an appropriate stretch target for improvement at an engagement survey item level. At a dimension or category level, where an overall change requires that you simultaneously increase results for all items within a dimension or index (or have the increases on some items so significant that they can offset declines on others, if experienced), a gain of 3 to 4 percentage points favorable is a more reasonable target for improvement. For an outcome like engagement, which is impacted by many, many things, a gain of 2 to 3 percentage favorable points may be a more appropriate target to set for a large organization.

You'll notice that we framed these targets within the context of "all other things being equal." This is because targets should not be set in a vacuum. Targets for the company as a whole should be set with consideration of the available external benchmarks. Targets for work groups within an organization should also take into effect internal benchmarks.

Of course, we want organizations to set difficult and challenging goals, but also attainable ones. Trust us, there is challenge in moving an entire, large organization a few percentage points annually or even bi-annually on its engagement scores! Also trust us when we tell you that specific, difficult goals that are attainable and thus accepted have the best chance of being accomplished.[12]

Actual Changes That Build and Maintain Engagement

Okay, so you've now fully prepared the organization for change and you want to know what changes to actually make. A preview of some of these interventions was provided in Chapter 3 where we focused on how to build and sustain a culture of engagement. Here though, we go into greater detail on the many interventions that can be taken to enhance engagement feelings and engagement behaviors. Which specific interventions are relevant of course depends on the driver analyses and the outcomes of the diagnostic phase. A summary of the proposed possible interventions is shown in the "Interventions" box.

Note though that here we are arbitrarily restricting our focus to interventions that influence the engagement level of current employees or prospective employees once part of the workforce. That is, we are excluding interventions that would build engagement capital through recruitment and selection practices.

Good to Know:
Interventions

Interventions that build confidence and resiliency:

- Provide success experiences for employees
- Provide complete information to employees
- Provide opportunities to learn – and to fail and bounce back
- Provide slack time for updating and training
- Provide performance feedback

Interventions that build social support networks:

- Provide many opportunities (meetings, training, informal gatherings, team projects) to facilitate the establishment of social support networks

Interventions that renew or restore employee energy:

- Provide opportunities for balance in employees' lives; do not expect continual engagement as such engagement can have a "dark side"

Interventions that enhance the motivation to engage:

- Provide jobs that effectively use people's skills
- Provide jobs and a culture that fit employees' values
- Implement effective on-boarding programs
- Provide jobs that permit autonomy of action and choice

Interventions that enhance the freedom to engage:

- Through trust and fairness from:
  - Supervisors
  - "The system"
- Repair trust if the "emotional bank account of trust" has been depleted:
  - Through fair processes
  - Through fair outcomes
  - Through fair interactions with subordinates and co-workers

Leadership as a central intervention in establishing a culture of engagement:

- At all levels
- Especially at the immediate supervisory level

Interventions that Build Confidence and Resiliency

The goal is to build the capacity of individuals to engage more fully with their everyday work. A key question is: How does the organization enhance the urgency, focus, and intensity of its employees? Recall that we positioned these engagement feelings earlier in Chapter 2 as reciprocally related to certain other psychological states such as resiliency and confidence. We indicated that success breeds success. As employees see that their best efforts contribute to positive organizational outcomes, their confidence and resilience grows, and more goal-directed energy follows. The key here is that employees need to experience success and that such success builds incrementally.

Some interventions address the problem directly; they focus on the informational resources that people have available to them whether directly in content or indirectly through contact with others. Managers should evaluate whether employees have access to high quality, up-to-date information needed to do their jobs and whether all employees know how to access this information when they need it. A broad view should be taken here; information comes in many forms and is not restricted to formal training programs.

A second form of intervention focuses on the benefits from learning and practice. People learn to adapt and bounce back from temporary setbacks through the experience of doing so. Also, confidence in performing very specific tasks develops through practice and feedback. Managers should provide appropriate practice in a safe environment for employees as they learn tasks. Organizations should ensure that managers and colleagues understand the importance of practice and allow employees to experience setbacks and learn from them. Building upon this, there is value in leaders and influential others sharing mistakes and setbacks that they've experienced and the key learnings that have resulted from these situations.

A third category of intervention focuses on making time available for thoughtful reflection which gives people the chance to reach out and discover or think through multiple paths to resolving problems.[13] When thinking more broadly than specific tasks, we also learn from our experiences in the aggregate; the repeated pattern of success in learning and practice extends our boundaries for thinking about how we can learn through practice and rebound from failure. Interventions that encourage time for self-reflection during learning and practice may further enhance success.

Interventions that focus on building confidence can have positive impact on factors that contribute to workforce engagement. For example, psychologist Sharon Parker has demonstrated that enriching jobs – long known to increase worker motivation – also increases the confidence of employees to take on broader roles.[14] Thus interventions focused on building confidence and resiliency directly impact engagement feelings and behaviors, by increasing role breadth and adaptability.

Interventions that Enhance Social Support Networks

Cooperation and teamwork are needed to accomplish goals, but the social relationships are also important in particular for individual engagement. Providing the opportunity for employees to build social networks helps to satisfy the inherent need all individuals have for relatedness to others. Beyond this though, working effectively with others fuels the motivation to reciprocate among team members. That form of social support also can enhance the psychological safety the team affords its members, which in turn reduces the degree of risk employees have when investing their energy in their work.

Importantly, social networks are the source of much of the information people need to do their jobs effectively. Thus, enhancing interconnectivity is an essential component of creating knowledge transfer. Organizational scientist Rob Cross and his colleagues have identified a number of methods put to practical use,[15] including:

- improving meeting behavior so that people feel safer to listen and contribute;
- mapping information flow to identify centers of expertise and providing that information so that employees can gain access to critical knowledge;
- enhancing opportunities to develop informal networks during employee on-boarding;
- holding "knowledge fairs" where teams can create awareness of the information they have for others in the organization and how that information can be put to best use;
- creating communities of practice to emphasize common vocabulary; and
- conducting informal brainstorming sessions to increase the frequency with which people interact.

These examples highlight the social importance of both enhancing information access and removing impediments that limit information flow. Some methods are clearly process- or procedurally-based. Others directly address individual behaviors that impact the quality of information flow, thereby influencing trust and improving the capacity to engage.

Interventions that Renew or Restore Employee Energy

A growing body of research demonstrates that recovery time during off-work hours is important to maintaining engagement levels at work. We will have more to say about this need in the next chapter where we explore the relationship between engagement and burnout. For now we just make the point, supported by research, that organizations cannot realistically expect or require maximum levels of employee engagement behaviors over long periods of time without opportunities for employees to renew their resources.[16]

Interventions that Enhance the Motivation to Engage

In casual conversation, managers intuitively equate engagement with intrinsic motivation. To them, the intrinsically motivated are engaged by their nature. We can't argue with the point, but it begs the question as to what mechanisms are in play, regardless of the labels we give them. Importantly, as psychologists Richard Ryan and Edward Deci have shown for many years, all people are to some degree intrinsically motivated in the sense that they seek to find meaning in their work and feel competent about what they do; they are "self-directed."[17] Some are more self-directed than others, but the general principles apply regardless of those differences.

You may recall that we have consistently found the opportunity to use one's skills and abilities to be a key driver of employee engagement. The empirical evidence we have accumulated through many applied research projects is completely aligned with decades of research on employee motivation and leads to the following basic and compelling premises supported by organizational science:

> All other things being equal, when people have the opportunity to do work in a way that: (a) effectively uses their skills; (b) fits their values; and (c) provides them the freedom to exercise choice, they will be fully "motivated" to engage in their work.

So, interventions that serve to build confidence and resilience are also those that help to enhance the motivation to engage, not just the capacity for doing so. However, also note our emphasis on values "fit" and "autonomy."

Values fit Engaged employees feel that their jobs provide avenues by which they can express their values, and similarly that their jobs are an important part of who they are. In many occupations this alignment of values can be accomplished through the work itself, such as doctors helping improve their patients' quality of life, social workers looking out for the well-being of families, and teachers educating children. While these are relatively obvious examples, many other jobs allow for an expression of values for some employees, though perhaps in less powerful ways. For example, customer service roles fit the values of those people who enjoy helping others.

Interventions that facilitate fit should therefore have a positive impact on employee engagement. Particularly critical to creating values fit is the effective use of on-boarding "socialization" practices. In particular, research indicates that values fit can be facilitated by experiences that expose organizational values to new employees.[18] As we began to note in Chapter 3 on engagement culture, the best on-boarding programs consist of both formal activities done in groups (e.g., company-wide orientation sessions) as well as activities done with one's manager and peers to reinforce concepts and make them more personally relevant. First, the overall mission and values of the company should be shared with newcomers, and these are best told through examples concerning real people to bring the concepts to life. Second, the strategic direction of the firm needs to be communicated as part of a formal orientation program, along with reviewing how the various parts of the organization together support this direction. This orientation is best done by the highest possible level in the organization – and in person, not by video. Having senior leaders present this information helps to highlight the importance of the message, but goes beyond this. It gives new employees, regardless of their level, an opportunity to interact with senior leadership. Third, newcomers' managers and colleagues should reinforce this message and make it even more directly applicable to the newcomer's role, explaining how their role (or the work of the group of which they are now a part) contributes to the company's success.

The optimal types of socialization interventions will differ depending on the nature of work and experience and skill levels of new employees. More generally, though, evidence indicates that institutionalized socialization practices are more effective in enhancing fit than ad hoc individualized strategies.[19] This in part reflects the observation that there are both "right" and "wrong" people from whom to learn.

Autonomy Prevailing views on work motivation share the significant view that autonomy is a central concept to goal-directed action. Simply put, the very notion of urgency, or goal-directed energy, has no meaning without reference to the possibility of empowered choice among alternatives. Of course, we say this as a matter of degree, not as an absolute. Employees who have internalized the goals of the organization and have autonomy in pursuing these goals will see their actions as being more a reflection of their choice rather than externally directed. Autonomy is a central concept to job (re)design and efforts to make work more meaningful.

A distinctive feature of job enrichment is the "vertical" expansion of jobs,[20] created by giving employees discretion over how they perform certain tasks. That autonomy can also extend to when certain tasks might be performed and how. At a more remote level, employees can be afforded the opportunity to contribute through other forms of shared participation and thereby influence decision making. For example, they might be given the opportunity to participate in team level discussions on work process changes or in setting goals.[21]

Not all people are equally interested in exercising control over their jobs. Some would prefer to take a more passive than active approach to their jobs. Thus, some people are more likely to flourish in an environment where they can exercise control and for others the opposite is true. Indeed, there is evidence from the field of Occupational Health Psychology that giving some people such control can create stress.[22] In the next chapter we will explore this more fully when we consider the dark side of engagement.

Autonomy can be influenced by interventions far less radical than job re-engineering. More to the point, it is important to recognize that autonomy is a matter of style and communication; managers can be trained to listen more effectively and to reinforce employee initiative. For example, managers can be taught how to give feedback in a way that is less directive and controlling. They can also be taught goal-setting techniques and the importance of giving employees autonomy in how they complete tasks provided that goals are met. Similarly, the importance of employees taking initiative can be reinforced in employment branding messages and in how performance is measured and rewarded in organizations.

Interventions that Enhance the Freedom to Engage

Our thinking on this topic can be summarized in restating our third principle of engagement introduced in Chapter 1: Engagement happens when people feel safe to take action on their own initiative. This is fundamental to our notion of building a culture that sustains engagement through fairness, trust, and psychological safety. We reviewed these concepts in much detail earlier in Chapter 3. From the change agent's standpoint, though, we offer the following principles that should guide any intervention:

- People make attributions about trust and fairness to the organization as if the company has its own unique persona. So, it is possible for people to think of their relationship with the organization distinct from their relationship with their immediate supervisor or any other specific individual.[23] This means that individuals may not trust a particular leader or manager, but they may trust the "system."[24] This implies that interventions focused on processes (e.g., fairness) can impact trust levels within the organization separate from interventions focused on individual leader behavior and relationships between managers and employees, such as are often the case in 360 degree feedback efforts. Put another way, it is important to differentiate process-based fairness interventions from relationship-based initiatives to enhance trust, with both types of actions having merit.
- The nature of an appropriate intervention depends on the initial level of trust that exists. That is, an intervention to "fix" a trust problem might be very different from an intervention to build trust, as in a situation where a new leader takes over management responsibility in an area. There is little research to guide prescriptions here although eminent organizational thinker Karl Weick tells us that prevailing wisdom indicates that it is more difficult to repair trust than to build it.[25] A more colorful way of describing the

problem is that leaders often don't recognize how quickly and deeply they dig themselves into the distrust hole – the trust emotional account gets depleted rapidly.

- There is risk in trying to repair trust. Disingenuous interventions intended to create the perception of trustworthiness may be transparent and can further damage an already fragile relationship. Nonetheless, organizations and their leaders face a dilemma. While efforts to repair trust through apology and explanation can be misinterpreted, Harvard leadership scholar Barbara Kellerman tells us that a refusal to address the obvious only serves to deepen mistrust.[26]
- What a leader does to build trust with one group or individual can simultaneously destroy trust with another. This comes about for two reasons. First, efforts to build trust by enhancing personal relationships with some can be seen by others as unfair. Second, some situations are inherently trust dilemmas because different stakeholder groups have different expectations for the leader's behavior or decision. It is precisely in these situations that people look to the leader for evidence of trustworthiness. This leads to yet another principle: Trustworthiness can only be developed over time and through circumstances where a leader's 'true measure' can be determined. [27] In the absence of such defining situations, leaders can only help to establish trustworthiness through efforts that build a reputation for credibility, benevolence, and integrity; they build the emotional bank account of trust. A corollary principle is that all the "little things" the leader does to build trust can be undermined by one act where employees see that act as representative of the "true" motivation of the leader.

In what follows, we consider two kinds of interventions based on these principles: (a) establishing organizational processes that enhance perceptions of fairness: and (b) the specific leadership behaviors that both directly and indirectly build trust.

Interventions Focused on Process Fairness

You can impact trust levels directly by focusing on organizational procedures. Of course, this begs the question as to where to begin. Again, survey outcomes can lead you to identify a starting point. As we suggested in the previous chapter, the survey can be designed to tap specific aspects of fairness (outcome, procedural, interpersonal). Procedural fairness questions can range from more general ("Decisions in this organization are made in fair ways.") to more specific ("The process used in this company for conducting performance appraisals is a fair process."). General comments collected as part of the survey process also can be helpful in targeting specific process fairness interventions. If your survey does not include the specific kinds of items that might directly lead to direct action planning, use focus groups to gather the needed information.

There are several characteristics of fair processes proposed by justice researchers Rob Folger and Russel Cropanzano that are worth enumerating because they point the way to effective interventions.[28] These include:

- *Voice:* Employees have an opportunity to voice their concerns and provide input.
- *Consistency:* Decisions are made consistently across people and time.
- *Bias suppression:* Decisions are made free of any personal bias on the part of the decision maker.
- *Accuracy:* The procedures in place should lead to accurate decisions (e.g., the assessment process for promotions should identify the best candidate; the performance appraisal process should accurately differentiate high from average from low performers).
- *Correctability:* The process provides for opportunity for unfair practices to be corrected through an appeals process.

Of course, managers can be trained on these principles. For example, you can:

- Train managers well on company policies and how to implement them fairly, including when and how to handle exceptions. This training should emphasize the importance of managers implementing policies in consistent, predictable, and uniform (neutral) ways.
- Train managers to fully understand that the interpretation of *what* they give to subordinates (in the way of raises, promotions, training

opportunities) is always dependent on *how* (the procedures by which) the decisions were made.

However, the focus should be broader than this. To enhance perceptions of fairness:

- Provide employees with opportunities for input into decisions that will impact them. Where decisions are made that are "unfavorable" to them, be clear on the rationale behind these decisions.
- Have a formal appeals process (e.g., a company ombudsman) where employees can direct issues of concern if they feel that they cannot adequately resolve them through other formal channels.
- Design HR and other systems with these principles in mind. For example, have skip level managers or HR generalists review performance ratings to try to ensure greater consistency, accuracy, and freedom from bias in this particular arena.

Interventions Focused on Outcome Fairness

Issues of outcome fairness may be thought of as both systemic (e.g., "The merit increase schedule in our company doesn't differentiate among performance levels.") and individual (e.g., "I didn't receive a fair bonus given my exceptional performance last year."). Systemic issues tend to rise to the surface because of other symptoms (e.g., high turnover in the sales group). Issues of the individual type are less evident and are clearly linked to decisions embedded in the context of individual relationships. We will turn to building trust at an individual relationship level shortly.

Importantly, interventions designed to address outcome fairness need to consider the "rules" by which outcomes are allocated. This strikes to the heart of sometimes long-standing conventions in organizations and therefore may be very difficult to change. For example, the compensation system in the organization may favor service longevity rather than performance during the appraisal period. The point is that the specific survey results or the follow-up to the survey results will point the way to specific interventions.

You may also note that outcomes are linked with process fairness in possibly complex ways. So, "issues" of outcome fairness can be balanced in some ways by process fairness. Put another way, employees will feel less concerned about a relatively unfavorable outcome when they feel the process by which that outcome was determined is fair.[29]

Interventions Focused on Interactional Fairness

Interactional fairness is largely created through the behaviors of individual supervisors, managers, and organizational leaders. There are two relevant features to this. First, interactional fairness is largely an attribution made to a specific person, and in particular, the immediate supervisor. Second, the implication for trust is that trust grows or declines as the relationship between the employee and supervisor develops.[30] This recognition brings us face-to-face with a critical conclusion about engagement: The freedom to engage is dependent on the leadership and management of the organization. It is through the specific leadership behavior that trust is engendered or destroyed; it is through specific leadership behavior that employee energy is released. We will shortly return to leadership behavior as a broader focus of intervention. We turn next to specific training interventions that can address fairness.

Training leaders to be fair Simply put, leaders can be taught how to be fair.[31] This is done by focusing on fairness principles. This can be embedded in training that is intended to address a specific issue. For example, fairness training can be part of programs addressing how to deal with performance problems, give feedback, on-board new employees, or administer and reinforce company policies. Such topics are staples of contemporary supervisory training programs. What we are advocating here as a specific intervention is to include specific aspects of interactional fairness principles in those programs. We have outlined the kinds of principles that determine perceptions of fairness earlier, and include factors such as truthfulness, respect, justification, voice, consistency, timeliness, and so forth.

Leadership Behavior and Engagement

Throughout this book we have emphasized the importance of leadership in creating an engaged workforce, and in particular, the role of leadership in creating a culture of engagement by both demonstrating trust and by engendering trust in management. So, in Chapter 1 we highlighted how engagement at 3M is facilitated by management candor and credibility. In Chapter 3 we created the framework for leadership interventions by describing how a culture of trust begins with senior leadership and is an outcome of specific management practices focusing primarily on building a climate of fairness.

All that said, it would be easy – and incorrect – to conclude from our emphasis on fairness that engagement simply reduces to a question of effective leadership. While it is difficult for us to think of a well-designed leadership training intervention as irrelevant, the relative gains from any one specific intervention have to be weighed against their costs and the other interventions that might also enhance employee engagement. For example, the gain from a coaching intervention focused on fairness and trust may be less than an equivalent or lesser investment in an intervention focused on job design. Interventions must be considered in light of the capacity, the motivation, and the freedom to engage. Nonetheless, there are specific leadership issues that are relevant to engagement and that serve as the focal point for engagement interventions. These are the interventions that create the foundation for trust – partly through fairness – and subsequent psychological safety.

Fortunately, significant research has demonstrated the impact of specific leadership practices – and specific leadership training – on building trust. The specific model of leadership on which these programs are based has been labeled "transformational leadership" and comprises the following very specific elements around which training is built:

- providing a compelling vision and a sense of organization mission and purpose;
- using symbolic gestures and emotional arguments;
- demonstrating optimism and enthusiasm;
- setting a personal example; and
- stimulating exploration of alternative problem solutions and new perspectives.

You probably recognize that these components tie closely to the feelings of engagement as we described them earlier. For example, part of transformational leadership is demonstrating the passion and enthusiasm that is part of the core feelings of engagement.

Summary

We've presented the logic of building and maintaining an engaged workforce by attending to the factors that build the capacity to engage, provide the motivation to engage, and create the safety and freedom to engage. It would be tempting to conclude from what we've shared here that "doing the right thing" will ensure an engaged workforce and all that an engaged workforce implies. Indeed, the evidence clearly indicates that engagement is attainable and not just an aspirational goal. We will see next, however, that the absolute pursuit of competitive advantage through employee engagement is not without risk.

Chapter 6

Burnout and Disengagement: The Dark Side of Engagement

Our goal in this chapter is to explain the following paradox: Too little focus on sustaining an engagement culture can yield disengagement – employees may withdraw psychologically or physically; however, too much of an engagement culture can also have bad consequences, including burnout, disengagement, and other negative psychological and behavioral outcomes (e.g., not adapting to the changes required for the company to succeed). Striking the balance is where the management challenge lies.

Efforts to improve organizational performance by enhancing employee engagement may fail and indeed may carry some risk. Some of the risk is borne by individual employees, some by the organization. The risks emerge because what employees are asked to share (in the form of their intensity, enthusiasm, persistence, and adaptability) comes at a cost that they may not be able or willing to pay. In addition, providing for the kind of environment that supports and maintains engagement has costs for the company. Some companies, when this reality hits them, are also unwilling to pay. Finally, disengagement or lack of engagement can result from conditions over which neither the employee nor the company has much control. For example, as organizational behavior researcher Terry Mitchell and his colleagues have documented, employees can remain employed with a company even though they are not engaged due to family pressures, social pressures, and commitments they have made that require them to stay employed in their present work place.[1]

The central questions of interest become: First, what boundaries we should place on our expectations for employee engagement, and second, at what point, if ever, does an effort to drive employee engagement become toxic to the individual employee and the organization? As we have carefully established in earlier chapters, a work environment that fosters and sustains employee engagement is grounded in a culture of trust. As in any relationship with such a powerful dynamic, there is the risk that one or both parties lose their sense of what is necessary to maintain that relationship. Whether that happens incrementally or in the form of a single precipitating event, the foundation for engagement is damaged, and the likelihood of continued engagement is reduced. Here are just some of the questions that emerge from the recognition that the state of engagement is "not forever," and may always be at risk:

- *If we ask "too much" of employees' energy and time, what are the risks?* After all, if our employees are willing to invest more of their discretionary effort, why can't we expect higher levels of productivity? Is there a cost too great for employees to bear? Is it the organization's responsibility to monitor the demands placed on employees? What happens when those demands are too great?
- *Is the energy employees display self-sustaining?* Or, does it require renewal? What form does that renewal take? Is renewal an issue of timing or form? Whose responsibility is it to ensure that opportunities for renewal exist, and that employees take advantage of these opportunities?
- *What do employees feel when they are no longer engaged?* What does it look like to others? Is disengagement unhealthy or healthy to the employee? What is the trajectory of disengagement? What interventions are successful in preventing disengagement?

These questions imply a dilemma facing organizations that need to draw upon the energy and resources of engaged and talented people, individuals who are engaged in moving the organization forward. So, we offer a corollary to our principles from Chapter 1:

> Engagement as a basis for creating competitive advantage is at a risk if the work environment is unable to sustain the engagement with which most people approach work. Employee engagement and well-

being are particularly at risk if work demands are sustained at such high levels that stress becomes chronic. Engagement is at great risk if: (a) the bases for trust between employees and the organization are compromised; (b) employees feel unable or unwilling to pay the price for being engaged; and/or (c) employees see an alternative work place in which they can again feel the positive effects of engagement.

This is clearly a qualified principle. Just like engagement feelings and behavior are not inevitable, disengagement and the dark side of engagement are not inevitable. Our emphasis in this book is obviously on building a work environment that sustains employee engagement. Our view is that most people will have high levels of engagement when the right conditions exist; importantly, the right conditions permit or facilitate engagement rather than pull it out of people. This

---

Perspective:
Working Hard and Long Does Not Necessarily Imply Engagement

Why do people work long hours? In a controversial book published in 1991, Juliet Schor suggested that the movement toward a shorter work week had reversed, and that Americans had begun to spend more time at work.[2] She attributed a significant part of that increase to economic factors and employer actions. While Schor's work attracted a great deal of critical thought, subsequent debate focused on whether the clearly lengthening work week reflected voluntary employee choice or the demands of employers, particularly in an era where increasing numbers of employees are exempt from overtime pay provisions.

What does the research show? As usual, the answer is complex.

People work long hours for a variety of reasons, in part including the psychological rewards, demands of their supervisors, the desire to get ahead, and social and occupational norms. Psychologists Jeanne Brett and Linda Stroh investigated several of these factors explaining why managers would make a choice to work 61 or more hours per week and they found differences by gender. Male managers who reported working long hours did indeed gain the most psychological rewards, and this relationship held after controlling for pay levels. Women managers who worked extremely long hours reported they benefited financially, but not psychologically.[3]

is not a subtle difference – it requires continual effort on the part of organizational leadership to ensure that the conditions that are necessary for engagement are actually sustained so that in turn the natural inclination of most people to be engaged is realized. Just to be perfectly clear: *engagement is not about asking for employees to do more with less, but rather, about releasing the full potential of employee energy when there is no need on the employee's part to guard or protect themselves from any downside to fully engaging.*

While probably unnecessary, we need to note that by engagement we *do* mean extraordinary or discretionary feelings and effort; we do *not* mean work characterized by long hours, misery, and impaired well-being, whether that follows from misplaced self-interest or organizational pressures.

Disengagement: Early Unmet Expectations at Work

Assume for the moment that most employees are engaged when they first join the organization. Some may be more or less engaged than others, but on average, they are predisposed to engagement; they are interested and look forward to a meaningful opportunity to use their skills, develop new relationships, and fulfill their personal needs. This is a very reasonable assumption. As we have suggested, there is very good evidence to indicate that people are by their nature intrinsically motivated, even while there may be some variability in the extent to which that is true. So, on average we can assume that at the time of organizational entry, people are inclined to give their best and not withhold their effort or energy.

But if people come intrinsically motivated what happens that leads to non- or dis-engagement? Why do some employees lose the zeal and passion they had those first days, weeks, and months on the job? Why do some become complacent, seemingly motivated to do no more than necessary? Employee surveys routinely show this to be the case; levels of both satisfaction and commitment decline quickly, often within the first months on the job. Quite often, we interpret such findings as evidence of a disconnect between what employees expect from their work and the company and what they find in reality.

Less usual is the following scenario: New employees encounter a work environment that is much more than they expected in the way of support for and social pressure for feeling and being engaged. In this case, over time, some times over short periods of time, employees "burnout" in response to various kinds of work stressors, distancing themselves from their work, other people, and the organization. They may appear to their co-workers to be distressed, and even contribute to the strain others feel within the work group. In these cases, as organizational psychologist Cary Cooper and his co-authors document, burnout may even lead to physical symptoms, including musculoskeletal disorders like back and neck pain and even cardiovascular disease like hypertension and heart attacks.[4]

We have described two kinds of disengagement: One due to the lack of support for engagement – lack of fairness, lack of trust, lack of challenging and meaningful work. The second is a function of too much support for engagement – the work is too challenging and even too meaningful (more on this later) and there is fairness and trust that cannot be reciprocated because of psychological exhaustion – a primary component of what has come to be called burnout.

As you can see in Figure 6.1, as job conditions become increasingly engaging, up to a point, the level of engagement rises – but then as those job conditions persist and even elevate, burnout emerges and begins the trajectory downward to disengagement. This phenomenon, described as the Vitamin effect by psychologist Peter Warr, explains why too much of a good thing is bad. That is, just as too much of certain vitamins is bad for you, too much of an opportunity

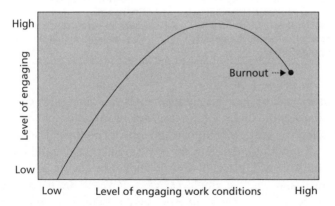

Figure 6.1 Engagement and burnout

for control, to use one's skills, and have variety of work can have a deleterious effect.[5]

By implication we have already somewhat addressed the first kind of disengagement: failure on the part of the company to meet employees' expectations for challenging work and a culture of trust. So, when new employees arrive intrinsically motivated and the work environment does not support it, we can anticipate frustration, dissatisfaction, and psychological withdrawal with many such cases resulting in actual turnover. In fact we make the following prediction: Company turnover rates are a direct correlate of early disengagement because of unfulfilled expectations for an engaging situation. As you can see in the box on turnover in organizations, the reasons for why people leave companies are dominated by characteristics of the work situation.[6] As we noted in Chapter 3, what this indicates is that early employment experiences of employees within the company establish expectations for their future with the company.

Good to Know:
Why Employees Leave Jobs[7]

- Dislike the job itself
- Difficulties with peers and supervisors
- Unfair HR practices
- Lack of scheduling flexibility
- Low compensation and little recognition
- Lack of career development opportunities

- Low employment security
- Poor job performance due to:
  - Lack of skills and competencies
  - Inappropriate performance standards
  - Lack of resources (training, equipment, supplies)

What may not be immediately apparent is that disengagement of this type impacts the success of the company in attracting job applicants. Thus, low engagement of present and former employees leads to poor word-of-mouth for the company – we might say the brand image of the company as a place to work is poor. The chance of attracting qualified and engaged employees goes down as the percentage of employees who leave goes up. And there is more as we show in the box on the costs of employee turnover.

Good to Know:
The Costs of Employee Turnover[8]

Wayne Cascio and John Boudreau who do research on the costs and benefits of human resources have detailed the expenses associated with turnover by distinguishing separation costs, replacement costs, and training costs. And, these do not include the costs associated with performance-level differences between experienced employees and new hires. They provide further detail on each of these as follows and we abstract them here:

- Separation costs
  - Exit surveys or interviews
  - Human Resource System updates
  - Severance pay

- Replacement costs
  - Job postings or advertisements
  - Human Resource System updates
  - Interviews, testing, and assessments
  - Staff meetings for decision making
  - Travel and relocation expenses
  - Post-employment internal notifications
  - Employment medical exams and background checks
- Training costs
  - New employee on-boarding and orientation
  - Formal training
  - Job-specific instructional costs

In short, companies that fail to create a culture of engagement for new employees or who fail to sustain this culture for existing employees will succumb to a pattern of low engagement, employee psychological withdrawal and turnover, lower productivity, lower competitive advantage, and a failure to attract the kind of employees they hope for. Such companies create an increasingly negative cycle of disengagement and failure rather than a virtuous cycle of engagement and success.

The Nature and Trajectory of Burnout

At this moment, you may be thinking that burnout is an overplayed notion, representing an extreme and thus, unlikely response. But consider the following three points:

1 While base rates are actually quite unclear, we do know that burnout is neither a rare event (published numbers in some

countries indicating an incidence rate of better than 1 in 20) nor is it specific to particular occupations (though the research history of burnout had its origins in human service workers). Self-reported burnout is much higher yet (see the box on Americans' report of stress).

2 Americans are working increasing hours, a phenomenon that first became evident in the early 1990s. Work stress and work hours are often discussed in the same breath and it is assumed by many that working long hours is harmful to people both emotionally and physically.

3 Burnout represents only the extreme end of a continuum. In varying degrees, many employees might be said to be at varying points on that continuum. While the relationship between work stress and the experience of burnout may very well follow a gradual unfolding process in response to *chronic* conditions, our understanding of that process will help to focus on what can be done to prevent the more extreme "dark side" from emerging.

Good to Know
How Much Work Stress Do Americans Report and What is the Impact?

In an October 2007 survey conducted by the American Psychological Association, 74 percent of Americans indicated that their work is a source of stress, up from 59 percent just one year earlier. Of employed Americans, 41 percent indicated they had considered looking for a new job because their job is too stressful, and another 18 percent indicated that they actually had left a job for that reason. Fifty-two percent of employed Americans indicated that job demands interfere with their family life, and 55 percent of those surveyed reported that they lost productivity to some degree because of work stress. Other surveys indicate similar results; several summarized by the National Institute for Occupational Safety and Health indicate that from 26 percent to 40 percent believe that they suffer from excessive work stress, and 42 percent of respondents in a Harris Interactive survey conducted in 2005 indicated that they are coping with burnout.[9]

Up to this point, our comments directly imply that burnout is a product of the work environment and, further, that it can be a product of seemingly very positive work conditions. On the one hand this may seem strange, as it is commonly believed that burnout is a problem of the individual employee, perhaps brought on by trying to do too much. In fact, the prevailing research evidence suggests that burnout is more closely associated with work environment characteristics than with individual personality differences,[10] although as we shall see, much of what we would need to know about burnout relates to the *interaction* of the individual and the work environment.

Looking ahead, we will first disentangle the components of burnout, and see that a state of psychological disengagement may be considered separate from emotional or physical exhaustion. In fact, disengagement in this sense may be considered an adaptive or coping response to that exhaustion. To be particularly careful in our use of certain terms, we reserve the use of the word "disengagement" to refer to a state of psychological withdrawal, rather than also including its more inclusive use of certain withdrawal behaviors such as absenteeism and turnover that might often (and do) follow. Most importantly, we choose to use the word disengagement as one implying poor adaptation to the work environment, a psychological state that is unhealthy, and not simply a passive response to an uninteresting work situation.

The Components of Burnout

Burnout emerged as a topic of scientific interest after it was first used in the popular literature and then became a part of our everyday language. We will use the term here to reflect the psychologist's meaning of the term. The most common definition of burnout – developed and expanded upon over a 30-year period by psychologist Christina Maslach and her colleagues – positions burnout at one end of a continuum with the other end represented by the feelings of vigor and involvement.[11]

Burnout is most often thought of as a state of exhaustion, of being overwhelmed with "no way out." It accompanies or is a response to high stress caused by relentless dedication to challenging work, and was first investigated in the context of human service occupations because of the common emotional symptoms displayed by those who are dedicated to helping others. More generally, though, burnout is not a phenomenon that is occupationally specific. Rather, it represents several conditions that are a function of the interaction between the person and his or her work environment. A description of burnout sounds very much like the exact opposite of how we framed engagement in Chapter 1:

> Work isn't exhilarating, it's exhausting. Rather than feeling enthusiasm, employees feel like they have to drag themselves into work every day. The people around them ask "what's wrong, are you feeling ok?" They feel increasingly detached from work as something that's meaningful. They may even feel that they no longer are competent at what they do. These feelings and the subsequent disengagement emerge over time.

We've made three points above that are consistent with cumulative psychological research: (a) burnout is experienced as exhaustion – a lack of vigor and energy – that has interpersonal, cognitive, and physical components; (b) it is accompanied or followed by a sense of detachment or distancing oneself from work; and (c) it has a profound effect on how people feel about themselves, i.e., their own competence, often leading to a loss of self-efficacy.

Strictly speaking, only the first of these elements is considered burnout by some, where the emphasis is on the loss of physical and psychic energy. The sense of detachment that follows from burnout may be better considered a coping response, and the loss of self-efficacy that sometimes follows may represent the natural response to a chronic lack of success. However, at least the first two components are generally considered to be part of the burnout syndrome in that their experience seems to be commonly associated.

The Trajectory of Burnout

Not everyone agrees on the timeline of burnout and its components so it is actually preferred to speak of a burnout syndrome: (a) a state of exhaustion; *subsequently* followed by (b) a sense of detachment – what we call disengagement – from work; and (c) *resulting in* less overt behavior that is characteristic of engagement behavior.

As we said earlier, there is more to the meaning of the state of disengagement than simple disinterest. Rather, disengagement, as part of the burnout syndrome, connotes a more profound sense of distance and loss of meaningfulness, as well as behavioral withdrawal from the job. The kinds of behaviors that might be described as encompassing disengagement in this sense include *indifference*, what those around the employee might consider lack of effort or even cynicism, an unwillingness to extend oneself either for the organization and perhaps even one's co-workers. The more popular press tends to focus on disengagement in its behavioral form, which typically includes employee turnover, absenteeism, and what some call "presenteeism" (i.e., present on the job but absent in spirit).

The difficulty in understanding the burnout trajectory is that exhaustion and disengagement are influenced by somewhat different factors. In particular, there is significant evidence that work demands are the general cause of emotional and physical exhaustion, and it is the exhaustion that yields disengagement.[12]

Where our presentation differs from many is that the burnout syndrome emerges out of the same work conditions as those, shown earlier in Figure 4.1, that promote optimal levels of engagement – but there is just too much of a good thing. Most who write about burnout write as if it is work stress that yields burnout, and we would agree, but the source of the stress – somewhat overwhelming engaging work conditions – is not as frequently noted.

The symptoms that accompany this state of disengagement are similar to those often described in terms of certain kinds of emotional illness (e.g., depression) but the research on this issue is quite clear: Burnout is not a psychiatric disorder. Such disorders are seen as chronic states of the individual, not due to specific and identifiable tangible work conditions that can be altered relatively easily.

Is Burnout Inevitable?

Burnout is not inevitable nor is it unique to specific occupations. Nonetheless, we mentioned earlier that early work on burnout focused on human service roles. A significant part of the thinking behind that early research was that burnout in such occupations followed from the emotional nature of "people-work," a factor that might be regarded as unique to those in medical care, teaching, law enforcement, and similar occupations, where there is such an emotional connection between service provider and recipient. The important issue here concerns the chronic nature of the meaningfulness and dedication that accompanies what can be at times intensively focused activity in the context of close emotional attachment.

Our own experiences tell us that providing service to others can be emotionally draining. Think of what happens when people are in the position of constant interaction with difficult circumstances such as working with people who feel troubled or are in trouble. It is to be expected that caregivers experience empathy with the very people they are trying to help. The weariness and frustration that can accompany that experience when efforts yield little in the way of progress (people die despite the best of care; patients fail to get psychologically well despite all attempts to bring about change), results in a very normal response: An effort to protect oneself from the pain.

One implication of course is that those who are most attached to their work are therefore most at risk for burnout. So, what we have are people who are fully vested in their work (i.e., they are engaged) and who nonetheless find themselves more and more detached from their work, and who find it increasingly difficult to maintain the energy to get to work much less fully engage there. As we have noted, this implies an apparent paradox: Those who are most engaged are most at risk to suffer from burnout.

It is perhaps easy to understand that people suffer from burnout under such difficult circumstances. But the fact is that people in all occupations can experience burnout. Nonetheless, the fundamental insights gained in thinking about burnout in human service occupations make clear the following observations:

- *Exhaustion results from the excessive job demands that people feel.* What constitutes a demanding job is varied, and can differ across occupations, jobs, supervisors, and work environments. It is not a simple case of workload but involves issues of challenge, meaningfulness, involvement, commitment, and so forth.
- *Disengagement follows when people lack the resources that are necessary to remedy or cope with the stress that even meaningful and*

challenging jobs provide. Despite their deeply vested interest in the outcome of their work, employees are unable to control the circumstances that create the extreme demands of the job. In effect, they are constrained by the nature of the job itself or the work environment. They do not have the capacity to control their own destiny, or the support needed from others in the work environment to help them cope effectively.

Both of these factors relate to the burnout syndrome in different ways, and the distinction between these factors makes it clear that burnout is not a simple construct, although it clearly refers to a loss of energy and the subsequent effort to protect oneself from that loss through disengagement. Indeed, the greater the loss, the more the individual needs to expend even further energy to cope. The ever increasing spiral of exhaustion and efforts to cope make employees ever more vulnerable to the felt demands of their work. The feelings of disengagement that result are likely accompanied by feelings of guilt and these feelings are enhanced when the employees trust their supervisors and have felt safe to take the plunge to feel and be engaged. As humans we want to reciprocate relationships with others when we are involved in a positive relationship that has been built over time. When the demands of work do not permit us to reciprocate, guilt follows, further increasing the sense of disengagement.

The question is: What makes for demands in situations that yield burnout and subsequent disengagement?

Good to Know
Do People Fear Being Exploited?

Not surprisingly, some people are simply wary of being exploited by their employers. Nonetheless, psychologist Robert Eisenberger and his colleagues have demonstrated that when the most wary believe that their employers are willing to support them, they actually demonstrate an even greater level of discretionary engagement behavior than their less wary counterparts.[13] As would be expected, wary employees who perceive less support are least likely to demonstrate engagement behavior.

Effective Coping With Burnout

We indicated earlier that burnout happens when individuals don't possess the resources necessary to handle the demands of the job. The resources most salient are those which permit the individual to exercise some job control over their work environment, or otherwise provide support, whether from co-workers or the employee's supervisor.

Social Support

The notion of social support to people has two meanings, either the perceived availability of others to help or the help itself. Not surprisingly, social support has a positive effect by reducing the impact of work stress. Less obvious are the mechanisms by which this occurs (the help itself being the obvious direct method). For example, social support can help to create a more positive work experience. In general, positive work relationships with others tend to raise the general sense of well-being that people have, and that counteracts the negative emotions that can otherwise accompany demanding work. Social support can also have a buffering effect by changing the perception of what might otherwise be considered a threatening situation. Knowing that others in a position to help are around changes the perception of a stressful work situation into an opportunity to work with others and share the experience.

For example, recent evidence suggests that under highly demanding work conditions, employees will actually demonstrate higher levels of discretionary work behavior that directly benefit co-workers, and less of those same behaviors that would directly benefit management and the organization.[14] Such co-worker focused discretionary behaviors can be interpreted as a coping mechanism targeted at strengthening the social support network.

The question is: How should organizations focus efforts on providing support to employees? The answer isn't always clear. For example, social support doesn't always have a positive effect. For instance, there has been some evidence that social support can have a negative effect on the perception of stressful events. This might occur if co-workers were to raise doubt about performance expectations ("I'm sure the boss wouldn't expect you to stay late!"), in effect creating role ambiguity, or were to convey alternate role expectations based on group norms ("No one else around here would stay so late; let's not create the impression that we can be pushed around!"). A more problematic negative impact of social support is when people receive support they don't want or think that they shouldn't need if they were more competent. That is, actual received support can be a negative experience when it comes at the cost of lost self-esteem.[15]

We believe the question should be reframed by focusing more on the components of organizational and supervisory support, and by answering the question: How should the organization demonstrate that it values employees and understands the issues they confront? The perception of supervisory and organizational support has been demonstrated to impact positively both directly on job performance and on discretionary kinds of engagement behaviors. More relevant for the moment, the evidence shows that perceived organizational support is related to lower levels of reported role stress.[16] The most critical component of support is demonstrating that the organization (or supervisor) values the employee. The relationship here is complex; when employees believe that the organization could do something about work-related stress but doesn't, there is also the likelihood that they will perceive the organization to be less supportive!

Good to Know
What Are the Risks of Burnout?

Among the most commonly cited outcomes of exhaustion are symptoms that are commonly equated to cardiovascular disease. Indeed, research evidence suggests there are multiple pathways by which burnout (and more specifically, exhaustion) precedes cardiovascular disease. These include sleep disturbances, tension, restlessness, inflammation, a decrease in immunity, and poor health behaviors. Other commonly cited risks of burnout include the negative spillover effects on family relationships and on job performance.

Autonomy and Job Control

Clearly, burnout is a debilitating condition with profound individual and organizational consequences. But why are we positioning burnout as the dark side of engagement? The popular view is that those who are most engaged, who have the deepest sense of attachment to the organization, those who are most motivated to achieve, are most susceptible to the negative impact of stressors in the work environment. As some have put it, "You have to be on fire to burn out," which we described earlier as the paradox of engagement. More within the psychological tradition, Peter Warr suggested that "proactive, risk taking people may be considered healthy in terms of competence, aspiration and autonomy; but their difficult relations with the work environment may also make them anxious for a considerable proportion of time."[17] What is not immediately apparent here is that the kind of employee distress that the engaged employee might feel is different from the kind of distress that a non-engaged employee might feel under similar kinds of demanding work conditions – more on the difference between stress and burnout later.

Similarly, research on the construct of core self-evaluation has shown that people who are generally positive; high in self-esteem and generalized self-efficacy, with an internal locus of control, and lower in the personality trait of Neuroticism tend to be engaged in and by more challenging tasks. They choose tasks that are more challenging, tend to achieve higher levels of performance, and are more satisfied in what they do. Similarly, they are less likely to be impacted by stress, and have fewer somatic symptoms. Research on the personality trait of Neuroticism (sometimes called by the opposite name, Emotional Stability) shows a link to burnout. More generally, both trait affect (positive and negative) as well as Emotional Stability are linked to positive subjective well-being. The point is that people choose where they will work and personality has an impact on where people choose to work. It also impacts how people cope.[18] How can we reconcile these seemingly contrasting theories and research findings? Arguably, those who are more self-determined and possess higher levels of self-efficacy are more likely to be engaged in their work. Why would more intrinsically motivated and self-directed individuals be more susceptible to burnout? Do they choose to be in more difficult situations by their nature? Or, are they more likely to react to stress under certain conditions? The former implies that the more self-determined are more likely to be frustrated by the nature of the work environment – a finding inconsistent with the stream of research suggesting that more positive people have fewer symptoms of strain. The latter suggests that the more self-determined are likely to be even more effective in circumstances where they are in a position to control their own work environment – the situation (high demand) fits them (drawn to a challenge, self-confident of their ability, and in control).

The evidence supports this position. More self-determined workers do not experience the same levels of exhaustion under demanding work conditions as do their less self-determined counterparts, provided they are in a position with some degree of autonomy and are in control of their work environment to some extent.[19] Similarly, workers possessing higher self-efficacy experience lower levels of exhaustion under demanding work conditions when they also have higher levels of job control. However, those who are less self-determined are more likely to experience exhaustion and become more disengaged as job demands increase.

In other words, the opportunity to exercise control over their own work environment doesn't help employees who are not self-determined to cope with demanding work situations, and may even contribute to the strain they experience. So, the capacity to control one's work environment is not an effective device for reducing the impact of work demands *unless* employees believe they have the temperament, skills, and abilities to meet the demands of the situation.

Burnout, Workaholism, and Engagement: Resolution of the Paradox

Nonetheless, we haven't adequately answered the objection (and the anecdotal observation) that more engaged types of people are more likely to experience burnout. We believe the answer to that apparent dilemma is in drawing an important distinction between burnout, workaholism, and engagement.

The relationship between workaholism and engagement is particularly worth exploring because in both cases it is assumed that the individual is working more (effort, time) than might otherwise be expected. Indeed, workaholics may actually create more work for themselves, although their motivation for this may be very different. Engagement behavior is self-fulfilling yet aligned with organizational goals. On the other hand, effort and behavior that falls within the workaholic syndrome is at times unnecessary and perhaps even self-serving, as when the workaholic refuses to delegate tasks that could be performed by others. Put in other terms, the extra effort of the workaholic serves a very different purpose than that of the engaged employee. Also, the effort associated with workaholism is not part of a positive work experience, but a negative one. Regardless, to the extent that burnout and workaholism are commonly related to perceived health problems and strained social relations, it is understandable that some would expect a relationship between extra effort and burnout, and therefore, the apparent engagement paradox. However, that paradox originates in confusion between the extra energy and effort observed in the pattern of the workaholic, and not the engagement that derives from intrinsic motivation of the engaged employee.

In contrast, engaged employees find their work to be a positive experience and associated with subjective well-being. They work long hours not because of job demands but because of the enjoyment they receive from their work. They find work meaningful and important. Moreover, the evidence demonstrates that there is a positive spillover of that experience to non-work activities,[20] the exact opposite of the negative spillover that occurs between work and non-work life under stressful work conditions. On the other hand, the evidence demonstrating a relationship between workaholism and strain is significant, although perhaps overstated.[21]

The problem is that to the casual observer it may be very difficult to distinguish between the two. Nonetheless, it is critically important to distinguish workaholic behavior from engagement behavior. Conceptually, the distinction is important because it serves to emphasize that engagement is not about asking more from people than should be asked or is fair. Rather, engagement is about creating a positive and healthy work experience. To that point, recent research by Dutch researcher Wilmar Schaufeli and his international colleagues demonstrates that workaholics work in less supportive social and psychologically fulfilling environments.[22] This can be understood in terms of the "strong, irresistible inner drive" that is a component of workaholism. So, knowing that people put in extra effort may not be an indicator of high engagement, but something far more sinister and unhealthy.

Job Creep and the Erosion of Trust

A byproduct of giving more to the organization is the possibility that expectations around the job can change. This is called "job creep" and refers to the (perhaps unintended) practice of redefining job expectations based on what was once discretionary behavior. The significance of the issue is that the motivation for the discretionary effort – reciprocity – is compromised. As a result, job creep can result in the employee perception that they have been treated unfairly, or taken advantage of. Thus, job creep is associated with an erosion of trust. Yet, a culture of trust is critical to the development and maintenance of employee engagement. Compounding the problem, there is evidence that inequity in the exchange relationship is itself a stressor, and a cause of burnout.[23]

Additional Stress Factors and Disengagement

Thus far, we've described burnout as a form of stress in the workplace that is a result of the demands people put on themselves to be engaged and to be effective yet feel a failure; that kind of burnout is the result of too much of a good thing. There can also be too much of a bad thing in the form of stress that emerges from various kinds of overloads imposed on people. Such stress is an inhibitor of engagement and can result in disengagement as well. It is very difficult to separate out disengagement resulting from too much of a good thing from disengagement due to negative characteristics of work situations. But disengagement of the latter form is not so much due to the absence of a culture of engagement as it is to the presence of a culture of stress. This culture of stress originates more from the unambiguous demands placed on people where there is a lack of choice regarding how they are to respond to role requirements.

While it is difficult to separate out demands imposed on people from demands people impose on themselves, it is worth noting that the literature on stress has identified a set of issues that make situations overly demanding and that can yield stress and disengagement. The following quote exemplifies these demands and their effects and makes the point about choice or the lack thereof clear:

Well, I really miss you guys … I'm afraid I jumped from the frying pan into the fire. In my new job, the computer routes the calls and they never stop. I even have to schedule my bathroom breaks. All I hear the whole day are complaints from unhappy customers. I try to be helpful and sympathetic, but I can't promise anything without getting my boss's approval. Most of the time I'm caught between what the customer wants and company policy. I'm not sure who I'm supposed to keep happy. The other reps are so uptight and tense they don't even talk to one another. We all go to our own little cubicles and stay there until quitting time …[24]

The research literature concurs; the following factors have been identified as dimensions or components of demanding work situations that result in stress:

- *Considerable work needs to be accomplished and/or there is too little time.* This is NOT a simple case of time spent at work. That said, all other things being equal, having too much to do is stressful and, when chronic, burnout can result. However, the evidence also shows that it isn't work hours alone that matters, but rather, the extent to which the hours (don't) fit the needs and expectations of the employee. Also, the consistent relationship between work load and burnout is confined to *perceived* work load; the relationship between burnout and objective measures of work load is only demonstrated inconsistently.
- *There is a component of pressure to display emotions inconsistent with what the employee feels.* This is one area where the research evidence does indicate that "emotion work" yields stress and disengagement.[25]
- *There is role ambiguity and/or role conflict about expectations for the work role.* Supervisors and managers may send conflicting signals about what is important; customer expectations can differ from management expectations. In the worst instance, personal values may conflict with management expectations.
- *There is a lack of support (from co-workers, the supervisor).* The person is essentially on her own to face a demanding work task. This may be considered separately from the issue of lacking social support as a coping mechanism.

- *There is a lack of fairness.* This is such a compelling factor that we have given it special consideration. A significant source of stress in the workplace originates from a lack of reciprocity between employee and employer, such that the employee feels that they have not received in kind for their contributions.

It is easy to see that some of these demands (including the perception of ambiguity and/or conflict among demands) flow from the nature of the work itself. For example, emotion labor is a direct product of the need to demonstrate certain kinds of behaviors in customer-facing situations. Similarly, time demands in some occupations are determined by external forces, such as the close of a trading interval in the financial services industry. The irony is that engagement is most valued in a context where it may be most difficult to sustain. As we have already seen, the dark side of engagement emerges when there is too much of a good thing; the kind of stress we discuss here is too much of a bad thing.

Remedies and Interventions

We have emphasized the fact that stress at work whether it be from burnout or work overload yields disengagement. This begs the question as to what can be done to counteract that withdrawal and depletion of energy, and perhaps in the worst case, how can stress, including burnout, be counteracted.

The Need for Recovery

In Chapter 1, we provided our first principle of engagement: "Engagement requires a work environment that does not just demand 'more' but promotes information sharing, provides learning opportunities, and fosters a balance in people's lives, thereby creating the bases for sustained energy and personal initiative." Research evidence shows that the more intense the workday, the longer it takes to recover. Moreover, the more demanding the day, the more likely that people will experience negative emotions at work. That's not surprising. What is important is that the intensity of the workday isn't dependent on just the number of hours worked, but also the experience of the demands during the day. So, what matters is the perception of how difficult that day is. On a related vein, all demanding situations are not equal, and the impact on the employee is not simply the additive effect of work-related stress.

Interestingly, work load has its impact on a day-to-day basis. That is, it isn't necessary to assume that only chronically high work loads create negative emotions. So, although stress may result from chronic exposure to job demands regardless of the source of those demands (self, job), there is a significant impact of the individual day on the employee's need for time to recover. Additionally, not all strategies for relieving the effects of stress are equally effective. The time to unwind is significantly impacted by the quality of leisure experience. In fact, research by Sabine Sonnentag and her colleagues demonstrates that challenging off-job experiences and not relaxation predicted positive affect the following morning (measured by feelings of being "active," "interested," "excited," "strong," "inspired," and "alert."[26] We emphasize the practical implications of this research because too often we fear that managers believe that occasional episodes of highly stressful work demands are okay. That logic confuses the fact that competent and challenged people are sometimes anxious in a demanding work environment.

Other Interventions

The National Institute of Occupational Safety and Health offers evidence of a number of different interventions proven successful in altering stress-related outcomes. Many of the kinds of recommended interventions focus on job and work redesign. There is a strong tradition of applied psychological research investigating the effectiveness of job design on performance, and the most compelling evidence is that efforts to reduce job demands can positively impact employee well-being; the evidence suggesting that efforts to increase employee autonomy are less clear. However, as we have indicated earlier, this can be understood in terms of employee predisposition to be engaged, an observation perhaps not as comforting as our prescription that creating a culture of trust promotes engagement across all kinds of people and groups.

Resistance to Change and Engagement: Another Dark Side of Engagement

Change in organizations is assumed to be facilitated by engaging employees in the change process – and the evidence shows that this is likely true. But why is it that some people do not wish to get engaged in the change process or even resist the change effort? Organizational change expert Warner Burke outlines the following reasons for resistance to change:[27]

- potential loss of the known and tried and true; and
- potential loss of the feeling of choice; that the change is being imposed.

We would add to this list of reasons the following:

- loss of a sense of identity in what one is actively engaged – the current situation and organization.

In other words, if people are actively engaged in what the organization stands for, what the organization does, and how it does things, then they may resist change because they have become committed to the current situation, which they personally feel is good and with which they feel involved. In psychology we have a notion of "escalation of commitment" that captures the issue quite well. Escalation of commitment is the idea that once we have put a lot of effort and energy into the pursuit of an outcome, we keep putting more and more energy into it even though objectively it will not pay off. We know this as the "keep butting your head up against the wall" phenomenon. Psychologically this is completely understandable because to quit we would have to say to ourselves that "all of our past efforts were useless so I must have been pretty stupid to do it." And it is this that can yield resistance to organizational change from those who have been most engaged.

Note that only some people who are engaged will resist change; those who see that the change will yield positive consequences for both them and the organization will become engaged in the change. What this tells us is that:

Organizations contemplating change must present the change and the change process in ways that make clear the positive consequences both for individuals and the organization.

Warner Burke puts it this way:

> In psychological terms, newness and the need to cope constitute stress. If the long-term rewards to be gained from the change are not greater than those enjoyed formerly, the stress costs outweigh the future advantage. If the new advantages outweigh the old but are not well understood by those making the change, again, the effort involved will not seem worthwhile. Only if the advantages are greater and are desired sufficiently to outweigh the efforts required to make the transition are people likely to embrace [engage] change willingly.[28]

How Should Engagement Initiatives be Communicated?

The question then becomes how best to communicate changes to improve the level of employee engagement. There may be a dark side to engagement, but that is perhaps better understood as confusion between what engagement creates and the kinds of apparent discretionary efforts and behaviors that are similarly driven by less healthy motivations understood as workaholic behavior. Simply put, it is always healthy to promote employee engagement when the focus is on promoting a culture of trust and then accepting the subsequent reciprocity in the form of engagement behavior. Emphasizing supervisory and organizational support practices that demonstrate concern and value the employee are always consistent with this perspective as are those actions that promote fairness. By implication, those actions intended to just get more from employees by design will undermine the very trust that promotes engagement.

We emphasize what is so obvious because the discussion of employee engagement and discretionary effort can be easily misinterpreted as an effort to get more from employees for less. Indeed, a 2007 article by Tony Schwartz and Catherine McCarthy in the *Harvard Business Review* said "To effectively reenergize their workforces, organizations need to shift their emphasis from getting more out of people to investing more in them, so they are motivated – and able – to bring more of themselves to work every day."[29] We see much of the engagement rush as easily misperceived as an emphasis on "getting more." To that end, we have noted that one very effective communications practice in some organizations is to *speak to* the importance of alignment between employee and organization, and to design action plans on the factors that create a work environment enabling and sustaining employee engagement. That puts engagement in the proper perspective, and promotes employee well-being as well as organizational competitive advantage. In Chapter 1 we provided context for this in describing how 3M leaders communicate through a variety of methods to deliver their message and in Chapter 4 we provided further detail on the importance of personal involvement at the executive level.

Conclusion

One might easily get depressed at all of these potential negative issues having to do with engagement. Our experience is that managers and executives who approach engagement just need to get a reality check on what they are thinking. If they are thinking this is a good way to get more for less, they are due for an unpleasant surprise. If they are thinking we can simply continue to raise the bar once we get them engaged, stress and disengagement and perhaps burnout will be the result. They need to think: If we do not provide the support and relief hard working and engaged people require, then burnout might be the result.

We obviously believe that an engaged workforce can yield important competitive advantage but this does not mean it comes free. It is just not easy striking all of the balances implied by working with people but those who get it right will surely profit – in many ways.

Chapter 7

Talking Points: Introducing or Rethinking Engagement in Your Organization

We've presented in detail a model of engagement that is based on the aggregate scientific knowledge that exists and the practical experience we have about what engagement is and how to make it happen. Our model is more than a psychological model; it is comprehensive in that it shows you what to do to take the energy that people want to give you and turn it into corporate competitive advantage.

Nonetheless, our experience in talking with many HR and C-suite executives is that they already have their own view of what engagement is and what it can do. We are typically told in the first few seconds of many conversations that "you're preaching to the choir." Then, as the conversation unfolds we and they learn that engagement is not really what they thought it was – and in particular just how different it is from being just another face on employee retention or employee satisfaction. Making the problem even more complex is that there is also often a history of thinking and talking about engagement inside the business that may be inconsistent with thinking about engagement as we've presented it here. Most often we hear about such vested interests in terms of comments like "Our CFO believes it's all about ... ," or "We have a history of doing employee surveys here and our senior team is very wedded to the items we've been using because they've been tracking progress."

We find that it is sometimes very helpful to reframe the conversation and even to avoid the term engagement because of the individual interpretations you otherwise have to argue against. For that same reason, we think it's important that the conversation not be one of whether to do "another employee survey" or "take the employee pulse." As we have positioned it, the survey is perhaps the final form of diagnostic that leads to intervention and action planning, but the survey itself isn't the point of the conversation. Rather, the emphasis should be on creating a culture that is consistent with building and sustaining an engaged employee workforce and, thus, corporate competitive advantage.

To that end, we suggest the following slide deck which is a brief 15 to 20 minute presentation (on average, 2 minutes per slide) of the key points we think you need to convey when you talk about engagement within your company. It is more than an elevator speech and it is less than a presentation you might put together for a major initiative. It also would require deeper editing if you have just 5 minutes of time with your CEO (think of 3 slides at most). Moreover, we assume that your audience has had some introduction to the engagement notion and your goal is to take that understanding further and to position a conversation around introducing an engagement campaign, not aggressively selling people on the relevance of an engaged workforce. We have framed this for you to use as part of conversations with your stakeholder audience whether individually or as part of a group meeting. Of course, you will want to embellish it; in particular you very well may want to include a slide that says how this is different from what you have been discussing in the past.

The Slide Show

Introduction

- When you think of the following characteristics that might describe our employees, what % of employee potential or available energy do you think we tap every day?
  - Urgency
  - Focus
  - Intensity
  - Adaptability
  - Persistence
  - Personal Initiative
- What % do you think our most significant competitor taps?

Figure 7.1 Slide 1: Introduction

Slide 1: Speaker Notes

Note that it's not about how much people give outside of work; it's about getting the conversation going on energy and what it is, what it does, and where it goes.

A discussion about engagement is about tapping the energy that people bring with them to work and energy over which they have discretion. Talking about engagement requires a discussion about what management at all levels must do to encourage employees to use their energy in ways that promote corporate competitive advantage; it must also focus on how management can help sustain that energy over the long haul.

Slide 1: Other Notes

You may find it helpful to mention that engagement as a conceptual umbrella is a useful way to understand and discuss some of the human capital issues that have always been paramount to executives, and in particular a way of embracing the more difficult to define subject of employee motivation. Most executives unfortunately think it is the job of management to motivate when it is really the job of management to promote the conditions under which employees display the motivation and energy they have at their discretion to use.

Introduction, cont.

- What do we envision when we think of the kinds of behaviors that indicate engagement?
  - Engaged employees persist – even when confronted with difficult obstacles.
  - Engaged employees take ownership for their personal development in ways that support the company.
  - Engaged employees adapt, are proactive, and even thrive under uncertainty – they aren't tied to their job descriptions.

Figure 7.2 Slide 2: Introduction (cont.)

Slide 2: Speaker Notes

These are all about the overt displays of energy that people bring to the job. It is persistence, adaptability, proactivity, and role expansion that lead to competitive advantage when directed toward strategic goals. Random energy is not useful. So, strategic engagement is a key issue as it is energy focused on what the organization needs to accomplish.

It may also be useful here to note that the focus isn't on employee retention, although that may be a byproduct of creating the conditions that create and sustain engagement. It may help to make the point that keeping employees isn't the high bar that the organization should be aiming for in a human capital approach to competitive advantage.

Employees want to be engaged. People want to feel competent and successful. People join organizations wanting to engage. We don't have to "create" engagement; we only need to find a way to release and sustain what is already there.

Organizations unnecessarily put roadblocks in their way and then wonder what happened to employee engagement. That is why engagement can only be released and sustained when supported by the culture of the organization.

Side 2: Other Notes

You can support this slide with statistical evidence relating engage-ment to financial outcomes such as described in Chapter 1. However, our own experience is that executives know or at least assume such outcomes in their own thinking. The issue here is making it clear that this isn't like other things they have thought about in the past and in particular isn't simply about employee satisfaction even though employee well-being is certainly an important consideration and very much an outcome of the kinds of initiatives in which you may later invest. Our experience also suggests that this is something not easily grasped or distinguished in the first conversation. Your audience may have significant predispositions about thinking of engagement as expressions of pride and loyalty so you may want to be prepared to discuss how those are relevant considerations and may even be byproducts of efforts directed at an engagement strategy. Take care not to let this sidetrack you in your initial conversations. Focus instead on what engagement is and what needs to be done to release it and sustain it, promoting the idea that many good things flow from an engaged workforce – including pride, loyalty, retention, and behavior that is strategically relevant.

```
┌─────────────────────────────────────────────────────────────┐
│ ▓▓▓▓▓▓▓▓▓▓▓▓▓▓▓▓▓▓▓▓▓▓▓▓▓▓▓▓▓▓▓▓▓                      ╲╲╲   │
│ Principles of Employee Engagement                      ╲╲╲   │
│                                                               │
│  ▪ Engagement follows when …                                  │
│                                                               │
│     – Employees see a purpose to investing their personal     │
│       energy – a question of motivation                       │
│                                                               │
│     – Employees feel psychologically safe to invest their     │
│       energy – a question of the freedom to engage because    │
│       they trust                                              │
│                                                               │
│     – Employees know what really matters – a question of      │
│       strategic alignment                                     │
│                                                               │
│     – Employees feel they have the support and resources to   │
│       contribut including the opportunity to renew their      │
│       energy outside of work                                  │
│                                                               │
└─────────────────────────────────────────────────────────────┘
```

Figure 7.3 Slide 3: Principles of employee engagement

Slide 3: Speaker Notes

Engagement requires a supportive and fair work environment as a basis for sustained employee energy and personal initiative and not just an environment that is continually demanding "more." Support and a sense of being treated fairly come from both the immediate individual leader and the organization; both are necessary. It is essential to think of what we can do to release and maintain energy over the longer haul. It is also important to recognize that much of where employees find support for using their energy is through social relationships.

Engagement happens when people use their important skills in a way aligned with their personal values. Engagement also follows as simple reciprocity for having been given the support they want – from having been treated fairly and well. The important point is that there is the need to treat people fairly, not just because people want to reciprocate, but because they will feel safe to use their energy without feeling that it will be used in vain on something unimportant, that credit for what they do will be taken by others, or more simply that they will be abused. Engagement matters most when ambiguity is high, adversity is clearly present, and when there is the call for change; it's also when people are most likely to feel insecure and threatened that engagement is least likely to emerge without the supportive environment we have described.

Strategic engagement happens when people know what the organization's strategic priorities are and why, and when the organization aligns its processes and practices – its culture – with attainment of those goals.

Feelings of Engagement

- Engagement is also about what people feel...and those feelings are the antecedents of engagement behavior:

  — Urgency – the sense that we need to "get this done"

  — Intensity – the sense of significance and deep level of involvement in what's happening now

  — Focus – employees direct their attention to what's important now, and not necessarily what's personally most interesting

  — Enthusiasm

Figure 7.4 Slide 4: Feelings of engagement

Slide 4: Speaker's Notes

The feelings of engagement are where some confusion can exist over what is engagement and what is satisfaction. Employee satisfaction and well-being are an essential characteristic of a thriving workforce. If we focus on doing the things that create engagement we will also create a work environment where employees derive satisfaction from what they do. People want to feel competent and be successful and they want the feelings of engagement not just the feelings of satisfaction.

So, to enhance workforce engagement, we need to think about how we create the sense of urgency, intensity, focus, and enthusiasm that lead to the behaviors we just described.

Engagement Requires Trust

- We earn the trust of employees when we...

  – Treat them fairly with regard to the rewards and recognition we provide to show people we value their contribution

  – Treat them fairly with regard to the procedures we use in managing them. For example we:
    - Give people reasonable flexibility when they need a favor or some slack because of personal circumstances
    - Adjust to employee needs and preferences
    - Keep people informed about why decisions are made the way they are
    - Give people time to recover from the strain of work

  – Treat them fairly with regard to all interpersonal interactions. For example we:
    - Ask people about their preferences and act on them when we can
    - Are behaviorally pleasant, considerate, and interested
    - Keep promises we make or even imply

Figure 7.5 Slide 5: Engagement requires trust

Slide 5: Speaker's Notes

Engagement cannot exist without trust. We earn the trust of employees, and this trust in turn creates the sense of psychological safety. If there is one way to describe trust, it would be to note that people are unafraid of feeling energized and investing that energy in their behavior. Such lack of fear comes from being treated fairly in all of the ways that fairness shows itself – and not only with regard to pay. In other words, we show people they are valued because we treat them fairly.

We also recognize people and earn their trust when we regard them as relevant stakeholders. That means we put their interests in line with those of others (not behind, not ahead) and we treat people fairly in every way as individuals. So, when we give people a chance to individually shine, use their talents, and express their individuality in their work we are showing they are valued and we care about their well-being. Doing an employee survey and providing feedback on and taking action on the results is one way we do this.

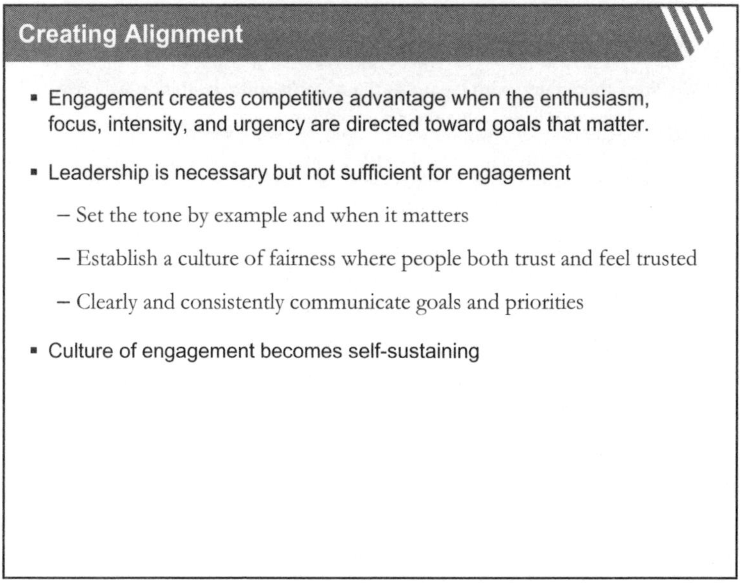

Creating Alignment

- Engagement creates competitive advantage when the enthusiasm, focus, intensity, and urgency are directed toward goals that matter.

- Leadership is necessary but not sufficient for engagement

    – Set the tone by example and when it matters

    – Establish a culture of fairness where people both trust and feel trusted

    – Clearly and consistently communicate goals and priorities

- Culture of engagement becomes self-sustaining

Figure 7.6 Slide 6: Creating alignment

Slide 6: Speaker's Notes

Leaders have to pick their opportunities to set the tone. It's not just a matter of communicating often, but also what they choose to do when they have competing multiple agendas operating and everyone is looking to see what choices and decisions get made because these are what really matter – communication is accomplished by the decisions that get made. Remember, the culture is set by what leaders pay attention to – especially when times are difficult.

When teams see being engaged as part of what and who they are, leaders are no longer alone. Teams who score high on engagement also have a high level of self-directed individual behavior reinforced by other members of the team.

The culture of engagement starts with leadership but the culture becomes self-sustaining when individual employees embrace the values of their leaders and the organization. At that point, the work isn't by anyone alone but with everyone. Engagement becomes about the "we" and not the "me."

Recommendations

- To have the engaged workforce we claim we want we must:
  - Validate we are on the same page and that we put into practice what we say is important at the senior team level
  - Define to our own satisfaction the engaged employee behaviors w wish to promote, that are likely to help create a competitive advantage, and that we accept as the definition of engagement
  - Ensure that we are communicating our strategy and employees' roles in achieving our goals in a consistent way, and one that shows we will support and value them
  - Identify and implement ways people can align their interests and their work – whether in the work itself or by building ways for people to identify with our mission and purpose

Figure 7.7 Slide 7: Recommendations

Slide 7: Speaker's Notes

The way we think about engagement and seek to build an engaged workforce needs to reflect both our commitment to business objectives and our belief that employee well-being is essential to that success.

We need to fully explore that we are on the same page by what we mean when we use the term employee engagement and how we expect that to be visible – to us as leaders and to our stakeholders when we communicate.

We need to be willing to rethink how we can build on what employees already want – a chance for reasonable autonomy and to gain and demonstrate competence in their work. We can do this both in how work is structured and how we listen to employees who have their own ideas on how work can be accomplished.

We need to invest in processes that ensure fair decision making and fair outcomes.

We need candor in our own conversations and recognition of our own shortcomings when we fail to live up to these values we espouse.

Recommendations, cont.

- Give employees credible leadership – both by actions and through honest recognition and acknowledgement of inevitable setbacks

- Create systems which build trust among each other and with our employees by emphasizing fairness and justice in our decisions, our procedures, and our actions

- Identify ways to demonstrate the seriousness of our intent – watch for potentially defining moments when we can reveal with trust and integrity that we live up to our values

- Monitor (and re-measure) employee engagement levels and take action on what we hear through employee surveys

---

Figure 7.8 Slide 8: Recommendations (cont.)

Slide 8: Speaker's Notes

See Speaker's notes to Slide 7.

Barriers

- We will fail if we...

  – Don't see this as a cultural change initiative but instead see it as another way of involving employees or showing interest by asking their opinions

  – Don't accept this as our responsibility yet establish local accountability

  – Don't communicate goals and priorities again and again

  – Don't embed our thinking about engagement in every talent management initiative we undertake –from recruitment to on-boarding to performance management

  – Don't make it safe for people to dare to fully live what we want, beit customer service, innovation, process efficiency

  – Don't demonstrate that we trust as well as deserve to be trusted

  – Ignore any legacy of failure in the past –we're not necessarily working from a blank slate

  – Don't give feedback and adjust along the way

Figure 7.9 Slide 9: Barriers

Slide 9: Speaker's Notes

There is inherent risk in undertaking an engagement campaign. From our experience, the greatest risk originates from less than a full commitment to making the necessary cultural changes. The efforts to make real change won't happen if engagement is seen as something to be concerned with during less important times, or as an HR initiative. The culture of engagement we want to create is something we must all buy into and accept accountability for.

Engagement campaigns, like all change attempts, require persistence, adaptability, role expansion, and personal initiative on the part of senior leadership – they must be engaged. If not, the engagement campaign will be seen as another "flavor of the month" that will go away soon so why pay attention to it.

Notes

Preface

1 Cappelli, P. (2008). *Talent on demand: Managing talent in an age of uncertainty.* Boston: Harvard Business School Press; Lawler, E. E., III (2008). *Talent: Making people your competitive advantage.* San Francisco: Jossey-Bass.

1 Engaging Engagement

1 Welch, J., & Welch S. (2006). How healthy is your company? *Business Week,* May 8.
2 Erickson, T. J. (2005). Testimony submitted before the US Senate Committee on Health, Education, Labor and Pensions, May 26.
3 The shareholder value index used is called Tobin's q [see Tobin, J. (1969). A general equilibrium approach to monetary theory. *Journal of Money, Credit, and Banking, 1,* 15–29]. See the description of Shareholder Value in the box on page 3.
4 Csikszentmihalyi, M. (1997). *Finding flow: The psychology of engagement with everyday life.* New York: Basic Books.
5 See note 3.
6 Kaplan, R. S., & Norton, D. P. (2004). *Strategy maps.* Boston: Harvard Business School Press.
7 Deci, E. L., & Ryan, R. M. (2000). The "what" and "why" of goal pursuits: Human needs and the self-determination of behavior. *Psychological Inquiry, 11,* 227–268.

8 Hackman, J. R., & Oldham, G. R. (1980). *Work redesign.* Reading, MA: Addison-Wesley; Deci, E. L., & Ryan, R. M. (2000). The "what" and "why" of goal pursuits. See note 7.

9 Latham, G. P. (2007). *Work motivation: History, theory, research, and practice.* Thousand Oaks, CA: Sage.

10 Porter, M.E. (1996). What is strategy? *Harvard Business Review*, November-December, 61–78.

11 Ibid.

12 Angela Lalor, Senior Vice President of Human Resources at 3M, personal communication, January 31, 2008.

2   The "Feel and Look" of Employee Engagement

1 Luthans, F., Avolio, B. J., Avey, J. B., & Norman, S. M. (2006). Positive psychological capital: Measurement and relationship to performance and satisfaction. *Personnel Psychology, 60*, 541–572.

2 Snyder, C.R. (2000). Hope theory: Rainbows in the mind. *Psychological Inquiry, 13*, 249–276.

3 Shirom, A. (2003). Feeling vigorous at work? The construct of vigor and the study of positive affect in organizations. In D. Ganster & P. L. Perrewe (Eds.), *Research in organizational stress and well-being* (vol. 3) (pp. 135–165). Greenwich, CT: JAI Press.

4 Schaufeli, W. B., Salanova, M., Gonzalez-Roma, V., & Bakker, A. B. (2002). The measurement of engagement and burnout: A two sample confirmatory factor analytic approach. *Journal of Happiness Studies, 3*, 71–92.

5 Csikszentmihalyi, M. (1997). *Finding flow: The psychology of engagement with everyday life.* New York: Basic Books.

6 Maslach, C., Schaufeli, W. B., & Leiter, M. P. (2001). Job burnout. *Review of Psychology, 52*, 397–422.

7 Kahn, W. A. (1990). Psychological conditions of personal engagement and disengagement at work. *Academy of Management Journal, 33*, 692–724.

8 Barsade, S. G., & Gibson, D. E. (2007). Why does affect matter in organizations? *Academy of Management Perspectives, 21*, 36–59.

9 House, R. J., Hanges, P. J., Javidan, M., Dorfman, P. W., & Gupta, V. (Eds.). (2004), *Culture, leadership, and organizations: The GLOBE study of 62 societies.* Sage.

10 See note 3.

11 Rafaeli, A., Ziklik, L., & Doucet, L. (2008). The impact of call center employees' customer orientation behaviors on service quality. *Journal of Service Research, 10*, 239–255.

12 Frese, M., & Fay, D. (2001). Personal initiative (PI): An active performance concept for work in the 21st century. In B. M. Staw & R. M. Sutton (Eds.),

Research in organizational behavior (vol. 23) (pp 133–187). Amsterdam: Elsevier Science.

13 See David Twiddy, "CEO uses customer service to drive Yellow Roadway to profitability" Retrieved June 24, 2008 from: www2.ljworld.com/news/2005/mar/12/ceo_uses_customer/

14 Pulakos, E. D., Arad, S., Donovan, M. A., & Plamondon, K. E. (2000). Adaptability in the workplace: Development of a taxonomy of adaptive performance. *Journal of Applied Psychology, 85,* 612–624.

15 Gwinner, K.P., Bitner, M.J., Brown, S.W., & Kumar, A. (2005). Service customization through employee adaptiveness. *Journal of Service Research, 8,* 131–148.

16 Crotts, J. C., Dickson, D. R., & Ford, R. C. (2005). Aligning organizational processes with mission: The case of service excellence. *Academy of Management Executive, 19,* 54–68.

17 Proctor, P. (2004). Shared destiny. *Boeing Frontiers Online.* Retrieved July 25, 2008 from: www.boeing.com/news/frontiers/archive/2004/february/cover.html

18 Haslam, S. A. (2004). *Psychology in organizations: The social identity approach* (2nd. ed.). London: Sage.

19 Retrieved June 21, 2008, from: www.google.com/support/jobs/bin/static.py?page=about.html&about=eng

20 Cappelli, P. (2008). *Talent on demand: Managing talent in an age of uncertainty.* Boston: Harvard Business School Press.

21 Retrieved June 21, 2008 from: www.jnj.com/careers/global/shared_values/employee_perspectives/index.htm

22 Locke, E. A. (1976). The nature and causes of job satisfaction. In M. D. Dunnette (Ed.), *Handbook of industrial and organizational psychology* (pp. 1297–1349). Chicago: Rand McNally.

23 Judge, T. A., Thoresen, C. J., Bono, J. E., & Patton, G. K. (2001). The job satisfaction–job performance relationship: A qualitative and quantitative review. *Psychological Bulletin, 127(3),* 376–407.

3   The Key to an Engaged Workforce:
An Engagement Culture

1 An excellent summary of the research literature on organizational culture can be found in Ashkanasy, N. M., Wilderom, C. P. M., & Peterson, M. F. (Eds.). (2000). *Handbook of organizational culture and climate.* Thousand Oaks, CA: Sage.

2 Schneider, B., Godfrey, E., Hayes, S., Huang, M., Lim, B. C., Raver, J. R., & Ziegert, J. (2003). The human side of strategy: Employee experiences of

strategic alignment in a service organization. *Organizational Dynamics*, *32*, 122–141.

3 As described in "Entergy employees return the favor." Downloaded February 20, 2008 from http://marketplace.publicradio.org/display/web/2006/08/28/entergy_employees_return_the_favor/

4 Terry Seamons, Senior Vice President of Human Resources and Administration, Entergy Corporation, personal communication, January 18, 2008.

5 Dirks, K. T. (2006). Three fundamental questions regarding trust in leaders. In R. Bachmann & A. Zaheer (Eds.), *Handbook of trust research* (pp. 15–28). Northampton, MA: Edward Elgar.

6 Report of the BP US Refineries Independent Safety Review Panel. (2007). Downloaded July 26, 2008 from www.safetyreviewpanel.com/cmtfiles/panel_charter.php?file_id=83&link_id=39

7 As cited in Berry, L. L. (1999). *Discovering the soul of service: The nine drivers of sustainable business success* (p. 143). New York: Wiley.

8 Covey, S. R. (1989). *The seven habits of highly effective people*. New York: Simon & Schuster.

9 Colvin, G. (2007). Leader machines. *Fortune*, October 1, 98–108 (the quote is from pp. 102–103).

10 McGregor, D. M. (1960). *The human side of enterprise*. New York: McGraw-Hill.

11 Ibid., p. 138.

12 Kouzes, J. M., & Posner, B. Z. (1995). *The leadership challenge: How to keep getting extraordinary things done in organizations* (rev. ed.). San Francisco: Jossey-Bass.

13 Northouse, P. G. (2004). *Leadership: Theory and practice* (3rd ed.) (pp. 40ff). Thousand Oaks, CA: Sage.

14 Lind, E. A., & Tyler, T. R. (1988). *The social psychology for procedural justice*. New York: Plenum Press.

15 Lawler, E. E., III (1971). *Pay and organizational effectiveness*. New York: McGraw-Hill.

16 Landy, F. J., Barnes, J. L., & Murphy, K. R. (1978). Correlates of perceived fairness and accuracy of performance evaluation. *Journal of Applied Psychology*, *63*, 751–754.

17 See note 7, p. 139.

18 Schein, E. (2004). *Organizational culture and leadership* (3rd ed.). San Francisco: Jossey-Bass.

19 Louis, M. (1990). Acculturation in the work place: Newcomers as lay ethnographers. In B. Schneider (Ed.), *Organizational climate and culture* (pp. 85–129). San Francisco: Jossey-Bass.

20 Schneider, B., & Bowen, D. E. (1995). *Winning the service game*. Boston, MA: Harvard Business School Press.

21 Roethlisberger, F. J., & Dickson, W. J. (1939). *Management and the worker.* Cambridge, MA: Harvard University Press.

22 Organ, D. W., Podsakoff, P. M., & MacKenzie, S. B. (2006). *Organizational citizenship behavior.* Thousand Oaks, CA: Sage.

23 Rousseau, D. M. (1995). *Psychological contracts in organizations.* Thousand Oaks, CA: Sage.

24 See note 23, p. 114.

25 Holland, J. L. (1997). *Making vocational choices* (3rd ed.). Odessa, FL: Psychological Assessment Resources Inc. (PAR).

26 Mayer, D. M., Nishii, L. M., Schneider, B., & Goldstein, H. W. (2007). The precursors and products of fair climates: Group leader antecedents and employee attitudinal consequences. *Personnel Psychology, 60,* 929–964.

27 Hackman, J. R., & Oldham, G. R. (1980). *Work redesign.* Reading, MA: Addison-Wesley.

28 Locke, E. A., & Latham, G. P. (1990). *A theory of goal setting and task performance.* Englewood Cliffs, NJ: Prentice-Hall.

29 Viteles, M. S. (1953). *Motivation and morale in industry* (p. 145). New York: Norton.

30 Anthony (Tony) J. Murphy, Senior Vice President, HR, Eli Lilly and Company, personal communication, March 13, 2008.

31 Macey, W. H., & Schneider, B. (2006). Employee experiences and customer satisfaction: Toward a framework for survey design with a focus on service climate. In A. I. Kraut (Ed.), *Getting action from organizational surveys.* (pp. 53–75). San Francisco: Jossey-Bass.

32 Schneider, B. (2006). Organizational culture is like red wine. In S. J. M. Reger, *Can two rights make a wrong: Insights from IBM's tangible culture approach* (p. 35). Upper Saddle River, NJ: IBM Press.

4 Phase 1 of Creating and Executing an Engagement Campaign: Diagnostics and the Engagement Survey

1 PepsiCo (2007). *Annual report.* Accessed June 20, 2008, from www.pepsico.com/AnnualReports/07/index.html

2 IBM (2007). *Annual report.* Accessed June 20, 2008, from www.ibm.com/annualreport/2007/

3 Tesoro Corporation (2005). *Annual report.* Accessed July 25, 2008, from www.ticker.com/Annualreport/TSO/TSO-2005.pdf

4 Nigel Martin, VP of Human Resources at Harrah's Entertainment, Inc., personal communication, February 5, 2008.

5 Becker, B. E., Huselid, M. A., & Ulrich, D. (2001). *The HR scorecard: Linking people, strategy, and performance.* Boston: Harvard Business School Press.

6 Schneider, B., Salvaggio, A. N., & Subirats, M. (2002). Service climate: A new direction for climate research. *Journal of Applied Psychology*, *87*, 220–229.

7 Colquitt, J. A., Noe, R. A., & Jackson, C. L. (2002). Justice in teams: Antecedents and consequences of procedural justice. *Personnel Psychology*, *55*, 83–109.

8 Fishbein, M., & Ajzen, I. (1975). *Belief, attitude, intention, and behavior: An introduction to theory and research*. Reading, MA: Addison-Wesley.

9 Tett, R. P., & Christiansen, N. D. (2007). Personality tests at the crossroads: A response to Morgeson, Campion, Dipboye, Hollenbeck, Murphy, and Schmitt. *Personnel Psychology*, *60*, 967–993.

10 Zohar, D. (2000). A group-level model of safety climate: Testing the effect of group climate on microaccidents in manufacturing jobs. *Journal of Applied Psychology*, *85*, 587–596.

11 Schneider, B., & White, S. S. (2004). *Service quality: Research perspectives*. Thousand Oaks, CA: Sage.

12 Snyder, C. R., Rand, K. L., & Sigmon, D. R. (2002). Hope theory. In C. R. Snyder & S. J. Lopez (Eds.), *Handbook of positive psychology* (pp. 257–276). New York: Oxford University Press.

13 Watson, D. (2002). Positive affectivity: The disposition to experience pleasurable emotional states. In C. R. Snyder & S. J. Lopez (Eds.), *Handbook of positive psychology* (pp. 106–119). New York: Oxford University Press.

14 Sun Microsystems. (2007). Corporate social responsibility report. Accessed July 25, 2008, from www.sun.com/aboutsun/csr/report2007/inside/employee_performance.jsp.

15 Modeled after Kim, T., & Leung, K. (2007). Forming and reacting to overall fairness: A cross-cultural comparison. *Organizational Behavior and Human Decision Processes*, *104*, 83–95.

5   Phase 2 of Creating and Executing an Engagement Campaign: Action Planning and Intervention

1 Macey, W. H., & Eldridge, L. D. (2006). National norms versus consortium data: What do they tell us? In A. Kraut (Ed.), *Getting action from organizational surveys: New concepts, technologies, and applications* (pp. 352–376). San Francisco: Jossey-Bass.

2 Kaplan, R. S., & Norton, D. P. (2004). *Strategy maps: Converting intangible assets into tangible outcomes* (p. 93). Boston: Harvard Business School Press.

3 For example see the following excellent books: (1) Church, A. H., & Waclawski, J. (2002). *Designing and using organizational surveys: A seven-*

step process. San Francisco: Jossey-Bass; and (2) Kraut, A (Ed.) (1996), *Organizational surveys: Tools for assessment and change.* San Francisco: Jossey-Bass.

4 See a summary of these driver analysis methods in the chapter by Lundby, K. M., & Johnson, J. W. (2006). Relative weights of predictors: What is important when many forces are operating. In A. Kraut (Ed.), *Getting action from organizational surveys: New concepts, technologies, and applications* (pp. 326–351). San Francisco: Jossey-Bass.

5 Church, A. H., & Oliver, D. H. (2006). The importance of taking action, not just sharing survey feedback. In A. Kraut (Ed.), *Getting action from organizational surveys: New concepts, technologies, and applications* (pp. 102–130). San Francisco: Jossey-Bass.

6 For a focus on the positive in survey feedback and organizational change see Cameron, K. S., Dutton, J. E., & Quinn, R. E. (Eds.). (2003). *Positive organizational scholarship: Foundations of a new discipline.* San Francisco: Berrett-Koehler.

7 An excellent source of current information on organizational change in general and change processes and interventions in particular can be found in Burke, W. W. (2008). *Organization change: Theory and practice* (2nd ed.). Thousand Oaks, CA: Sage

8 See note 5.

9 Alderfer, C. P., & Brown, L. D. (1972). Designing an "empathic question-naire" for organizational research. *Journal of Applied Psychology, 56,* 456–460.

10 Klein, K. J., Conn, A. B., & Sorra, J. S. (2001). Implementing computerized technology: An organizational analysis. *Journal of Applied Psychology, 86,* 811–824.

11 Zohar, D. (2000). A group-level model of safety climate: Testing the effect of group climate on microaccidents in manufacturing jobs. *Journal of Applied Psychology, 85,* 587–596.

12 Locke, E. A., & Latham, G. P. (1990). *A theory of goal setting and task performance.* Englewood Cliffs, NJ: Prentice-Hall.

13 Sutcliffe, K. M., & Vogus, T. J. (2003) Organizing for resilience. In K. S. Cameron, J. E. Dutton, & R. E. Quinn (Eds.), *Positive organizational scholarship* (pp. 94–110). San Francisco: Berrett-Koehler.

14 Parker, S. K. (1998). Enhancing role breadth self-efficacy: The roles of job enrichment and other organizational interventions. *Journal of Applied Psychology, 83,* 835–852.

15 Cross, R., Parker, A., Prusak, L., & Borgatti, S. P. (2001). Knowing what we know: Supporting knowledge creation and sharing in social networks. *Organizational Dynamics, 30,* 100–120.

16 Schaufeli, W. B., & Bakker, A. B. (2004). Job demands, job resources and their relationship with burnout and engagement: A multi-sample study. *Journal of Organizational Behavior*, 25, 293–315.

17 Ryan, R. M., & Deci, E. L. (2000). Self-determination theory and the facilitation of intrinsic motivation, social development, and well-being. *American Psychologist*, 55, 68–78.

18 Kammeyer-Mueller, J. D. (2007). The dynamics of newcomer adjustment: Dispositions, context, interactions and fit. In C. Ostroff & T. A. Judge (Eds.), *Perspectives on organizational fit* (pp. 99–122). New York: Erlbaum.

19 Cooper-Thomas, H., & Anderson, N. (2002). Newcomer adjustment: The relationship between organizational socialization tactics, information acquisition and attitudes. *Journal of Occupational and Organizational Psychology*, 75, 423–437.

20 Hackman, J. R., & Oldham, G. (1976). Motivation through the design of work: Test of a theory. *Organizational Behavior and Human Performance*, 16, 250–279.

21 See note 14.

22 Meier, L. L, Semmer, N. K., Elfering, A., & Jacobshagen, N. (2008). The double meaning of control: Three-way interactions between internal resources, job control, and stressors at work. *Journal of Occupational Health Psychology*, 13(3), 244–258.

23 Rhoades, L., & Eisenberger, R. (2002). Perceived organizational support: A review of the literature. *Journal of Applied Psychology*, 87, 698—71z4.

24 Dirks, K. T. (2006). Three fundamental questions regarding trust in leaders. In R. Bachmann & A. Zaheer (Eds.), *Handbook of trust research* (pp. 15–28). Northampton, MA: Elgar.

25 Dirks, K. T., Lewicki, R.J., & Zaheer, A. (2008). Repairing relationships within and between organizations: Building a conceptual foundation. *Academy of Management Review*, 34, 68–84; Weick, K. E. (2008). Trust: A bigger picture. *Academy of Management Review*, 31, 271–274.

26 Kellerman, B. (2006). When should a leader apologize – and when not? *Harvard Business Review*, 84(4), 72–81.

27 See note 24.

28 Folger, R., & Cropanzano, R. (1998). *Organizational justice and human resources management*. Thousand Oaks, CA: Sage.

29 Brockner, J., & Wiesenfeld, B. (2005). How, when, and why does outcome favorability interact with procedural fairness? In G. Greenburg and J. Colquitt (Eds.), *Handbook of organizational justice* (pp. 525–553). Mahwah, NJ: Erlbaum.

30 Lewicki, R. J., Wiethoff, C., & Tomlinson, E. C. (2005). What is the role of trust in organizational justice? In G. Greenburg and J. Colquitt (Eds.), *Handbook of organizational justice*. Mahwah (pp. 247–270), NJ: Erlbaum.

31 Brockner, J (2006). Why is it so hard to be fair? *Harvard Business Review, 84*(3), 122–129.

6 Burnout and Disengagement: The Dark Side of Engagement

1 Mitchell, T. R., Holtom, B. C., Lee, T. W., Sablynzki, C. J., & Erez, M. (2001). Why people stay: Using job embeddedness to predict voluntary turnover. *Academy of Management Journal, 44*, 1102–1121.

2 Schor, J. (1991). *The overworked American: The unexpected decline of leisure.* New York: Basic Books.

3 Brett, J. M., & Stroh, L. K. (2003). Working 61 plus hours a week: Why do managers do it? *Journal of Applied Psychology, 88*, 67–78.

4 Cooper, C. L., Dewe, P. J., & O'Driscoll, M. P. (2001). *Organizational stress: A review and critique of theory, research, and applications.* Thousand Oaks, CA: Sage.

5 Warr, P. (1994). A conceptual framework for the study of work and mental health. *Work & Stress, 8*, 84–97.

6 Jackson, S. E., & Schuler, R. S. (2003). *Managing human resources through strategic partnerships* (8th ed.) (p. 286). Cincinnati, OH: South-Western.

7 Ibid.

8 Abstracted from Cascio, W., & Boudreau, J. (2008). *Investing in people.* Upper Saddle River, NJ: FT Press.

9 Accessed July 22, 2008 from www.concoursgroup.com/publications/EEE_011905_PressRelease.pdf

10 Melamed, S., Shirom, A., Toker, S., Berliner, S., & Shapira, I. (2006). Burnout and risk of cardiovascular disease: Evidence, possible causal paths, and promising research directions. *Psychological Bulletin, 132*, 327–353.

11 Maslach, C., Schaufeli, W. B., & Leiter, M. P. (2001). Job burnout. *Review of Psychology, 52*, 397–422.

12 Halbesleben, J. R. B., & Buckley, R. M. (2004). Burnout in organizational life. *Journal of Management, 30*, 859–879.

13 Lynch, P. D., Eisenberger, R., & Armeli, S. (1999). Perceived organizational support: Inferior versus superior performance by wary employees. *Journal of Applied Psychology, 84*, 467–483.

14 Halbesleben, J. R. B., & Bowler, W. M. (2007). Emotional exhaustion and job performance: The mediating role of motivation. *Journal of Applied Psychology, 92*, 93–106.

15 See note 12.

16 Rhoades, L., & Eisenberger, R. (2002). Perceived organizational support: A review of the literature. *Journal of Applied Psychology, 87*, 698–714.

17 See note 5.

18 George, J. M., & Brief, A. P. (2004). Personality and work-related distress. In B. Schneider & D. B. Smith (Eds.), *Personality and organizations* (pp. 193–219). Mahwah, NJ: Erlbaum.

19 Fernet, C., Guay, F., & Senecal, C. (2004). Adjusting to job demands: The role of work self-determination and job control in predicting burnout. *Journal of Vocational Behavior, 65,* 39–56.

20 Schaufeli, W. B., Taris, T. W., & van Rhenen, W. (2008). Workaholism, burnout, and work engagement: Three of a kind or three different kinds of employee well-being? *Applied Psychology, 57,* 173–203.

21 McMillan, L. H. W., & O'Driscoll, M. P. (2004). Workaholism and health: Implications for organizations. *Journal of Organizational Change Management, 17,* 509–519.

22 See note 20.

23 Taris, T. W., Peeters, M. C. W., LeBlanc, P.M., Schreurs, P. J. G., & Schaufeli, W. B. (2001). From inequity to burnout: The role of job stress. *Journal of Occupational Health Psychology, 6,* 303–323.

24 National Institute for Occupational Safety and Health. (1999). *Stress … at work.* (US Department of Health and Human Services. Publication 99–101). Accessed on December 19, 2008 from www.cdc.gov/niosh/stresswk.html

25 Grandey, A. A., & Brauburger, A. L. (2002). The emotion regulation behind the customer service smile. In R. G. Lord, R. J. Klimoski, & R. Kanfer (Eds.), *Emotions in the workplace* (pp 260–294). San Francisco: Jossey-Bass.

26 Sonnentag, S., Binnewies, C., & Mojza, E. J. (2008). "Did you have a nice evening?" A day-level study of recovery experiences, sleep, and affect. *Journal of Applied Psychology, 93,* 674–684.

27 Burke, W. W. (2008). *Organization change: Theory and practice* (2nd ed.). Thousand Oaks, CA: Sage.

28 Ibid.

29 Schwartz, T., & McCarthy, C. (2007). Manage your energy, not your time. *Harvard Business Review, 85,* 63–66, 68, 70–73.

Author and Name Index

Authors cited in references to published works are listed as well as the names of people who are quoted and/or who contributed in other ways to the development of the book.

Ajzen, I. 93, 180n8
Alderfer, C.P. 181n9
Anderson, N. 182n19
Arad, S. 177n14
Armeli, S. 183n13
Ashkanasy, N.M. 177n1
Avey, J.B. 176n1
Avolio, B.J. 176n1

Bachmann, R. 178n5, 182n24
Bakker, A.B. 176n4, 182n16
Barnes, J.L. 178n16
Barsade, S.G. 176n8
Becker, B.E. 91, 179n5
Berliner, S. 183n10
Berry, L.L. 55, 178n7
Binnewies, C. 184n26
Bitner, M.J. 177n15
Bono, J.E. 177n23
Borgatti, S.P. 181n15
Boudreau, J. 143, 183n8

Bowen, D.E. 178n20
Bowler, W.M. 183n14
Brauburger, A.L. 184n25
Brett, J. M. 139, 183n3
Brief, A.P. 184n18
Brockner, J. 182n29, 183n31
Brown, L.D. 181n9
Brown, S.W. 177n15
Buckley, R.M. 183n12
Burke, W.W. 159, 160, 181n7, 184n27

Cameron, K.S. 181n6, 181n13
Campion, M.A. 180n9
Cappelli, P. 175n1, 177n20
Cascio, W. 143, 183n8
Chenault, K. 50
Christiansen, N.D. 180n9
Church, A.H. 112, 114, 180n3, 181n5
Colquitt, J. 180n7, 182n29, 182n30

185

Subject Index